# THE CONTRARY FARMER'S
# INVITATION TO GARDENING

## The Garden Alliance

The Garden Alliance consists of companies and organizations supportive of the practices of organic gardening and the principles of sustainable living. Charter members of the Alliance are:

 Johnny's Selected Seeds
Albion, Maine

 Seeds of Change
Santa Fe, New Mexico

 NOFA (Northeast Organic Farming Association)
Richmond, Vermont

 Gardener's Supply Company
Burlington, Vermont

For more information on the Garden Alliance, see the end of the book.

# GENE LOGSDON

# THE CONTRARY FARMER'S

## *Invitation to Gardening*

CHELSEA GREEN PUBLISHING COMPANY
WHITE RIVER JUNCTION, VERMONT

Book design by Kate Mueller, Electric Dragon Productions
Cover illustration by George Lawrence, copyright © 1996

Printed in the United States of America

99    98    97    1    2    3    4    5

Chelsea Green Publishing Company
P.O. Box 428
White River Junction, Vermont 09001


Library of Congress Cataloging-in-Publication Data

Logsdon, Gene.
    The contrary farmer's invitation to gardening / Gene Logsdon
        p.    cm.
    Includes index.
    ISBN 0-930031-96-2
        1. Gardening.    2. Farm life.    3. Logsdon, Gene.    4. Gardening—
    United States.    5. Farm life—United States.    I. Title
    SB455.3.L64    1997
    635—dc21                                                    97-5790

A toast to Chelsea Green to whom I dedicate this book. May its banner wave forever over the green and graceful earth it champions.

# CONTENTS

# THE CONTRARY FARMER'S
# INVITATION TO GARDENING

# CHAPTER 1

# THE ECONOMY OF EDEN

*I have learned how to grow healthy crops without the slightest help from mycologists, entomologists, bacteriologists, agricultural chemists, statisticians, spraying machines, insecticides, germicides, and all the other expensive paraphernalia of the modern experiment station.*

Sir Albert Howard, in his *An Agricultural Testament*
(first published in 1940)

If Albert Howard (ironically a mycologist himself) had gone on to write that he had also learned how to grow healthy crops without any help from politicians, economists, churchmen, government subsidies, oil companies, PACs, and charitable foundations—up the gazoo to the lot of them—he would then have written the perfect Declaration of Food Independence for the 21st century. For in truth, none of these experts are necessary to the production of food and fiber. We know how to to grow healthy crops from the experience of intelligent gardeners and farmers, now and for centuries immemorial. That experience is our best science. There is no big mystery to it. We also know how to craft houses and furniture and clothes and musical instruments and tools without any help from the above-mentioned offices, which are more often merely bureaucratic cubbyholes, as Howard described them, where cunning little minds spend their days justifying their existence—parasites on the body of science and the body politic. Howard knew. He was trying to work through the British bureaucracy in India to help that country's small farmers attain a sustainable, self-reliant, independent food production system—Gandhi's dream. But he soon realized that "help" from the bureaucracy was not needed.

Nor is it today. In America, governmental "help" has only helped separate societies from the necessary knowledge of taking care of themselves. Abraham Lincoln's most naive belief was that people needed a bureaucracy to help them grow food, which is why he created the Department of Agriculture. Now an entire two generations of Americans are totally dependent on an oligarchy of greedy agribusiness tycoons for their very survival.

Knowledge from our current coterie of university magicians is vastly overrated. The man who built our house never went to college—never read a book, to my knowledge—but you will look long and hard for a house as well-built for the money. With all our vaunted technological expertise, we are not even sure how people built the pyramids. I doubt that even one farmer or gardener in the U.S. has ever studied the wondrously sophisticated, irrigated garden farms of ancient Mexico, ancient Cambodia, ancient Africa, and ancient Babylon, nor the marvelous blend of agriculture and hunting-gathering practiced by the Hopewell mound-building cultures of the American Corn Belt, all enduring for centuries without even a whisper from any land-grant college.

I am not a revolutionary; I utter only a plain truth. My wife and I produce most of our food, and some for our children's families, using knowledge we gained from our parents, and they from their parents, and they from their parents. Not a one of our forebears ever cracked an agronomic textbook or knew the Latin name of a single plant. My father and mother and both grandfathers and grandmothers and my father-in-law and mother-in-law all held agricultural extension advisors in disdain. Tradition, supplemented by our own experience and that of other gardeners and farmers, has been the key to our food-growing success. Thousands of books by gardeners and farmers pass this knowledge on to anyone who wants it. To this day, after forty years of avidly reading and searching the realms of "modern" agriculture for information, I have found little knowledge beyond oral tradition that helps us produce food any better. And a whole lot that encourages us to produce it worser. The keys to agricultural success, apart from common sense, were articulated by Virgil, and he got them from the Greeks, who in turn got them from the Orient, where for forty centuries China supported a population far denser than ours today, with gardens. And for the most part, China and all the East still supports itself primarily by the kind of small farms that in the U.S. the Census Bureau is trying to define out of existence.

This kind of gardening is not the effete horticulture of the wealthier classes as showcased in *House and Garden,* not Marie Antoinette herding a few sheep on her castle lawn or Louis XIV growing orange trees in his Versailles glasshouses while the people of France starved. Rather, think of the garden plots of the Russian peasants who have kept their country from collapse during fifty years of state-run agri-mania. Think of the food gardens blossoming in the rotted cores of big American cities. Think of the Dutch tearing up sidewalks to plant vegetables.

Having observed modern agribusiness for fifty years and having been personally involved in that world for much of that time, I am convinced that the present rush to industrialized farms and animal factories of almost unimaginable size cannot sustain itself, and that economics will force a downsizing, as it has in other bloated businesses. The only reason downsizing hasn't occurred in animal factories is because of the frightfully low wages paid in them. If downsizing does occur, it seems to me entirely possible that because of shifts already in motion, the food garden and backyard orchard (broadly defined to include small-scale husbandry and forestry) are capable of taking up enough slack to stave off a serious food crisis.

A Declaration of Food Independence such as I suggest would foster and be dependent upon a deeper and more profound declaration of *interdependence*—and a new economy. A nation made up primarily of garden farms would mean a realignment of people into smaller and more local trade complexes. This "distributive economy," to use the phrase popularized in the 1930s and 1940s when many people began questioning both capitalism and socialism, would be based upon personal contact between consumer and producer, and upon biological technologies more than on machine technologies—the economy of Eden, in other words. Then humans would understand that people mattered, and not only people, but all living things upon which people depend. Common interest and self-interest would become one, and that is the definition of a real community.

I don't think that this is a dreamer's utopian vision. Japan, on the basis of an average farm size of under ten acres, has become one of the most powerful countries, financially speaking, in the world. Now that Japan is trying to consolidate its farms, guess what? Its money economy has turned fickle. We forget that Japan's march to economic eminence began after World War II, when the United States dispossessed nonfarming landlords of five million acres and gave it back to the peasants. All of Asia thrives on an economy supported by the world's largest number of small shopkeepers, per capita. In America we are groping in that direction (in part from the influence of Asian immigrants). Many millions of gardeners and an unknown number of garden farmers (about five million, by my guess), some so small that they are not counted as farmers by the U.S. census, are out there working unwittingly toward a new decentralized economy.

I don't rely on sociological statistics or economists' models (talk about visionary!) to say this. As a reclusive writer of minor books, I've been receiving an average of two letters or phone calls each week from these gardeners and farmers all over the nation. I can tell you that there are a whole lot of people in this country who don't swallow the promises of either the capitalistic or socialistic economists anymore.

And I don't come to my notion of garden farming as a new economic (if not political) movement from reading the *Wall Street Journal* and *In Business* magazine, which are full of stories supporting a trend to decentralization, but from attending classes in my chicken coop for fifty years. My little red hens understand the meaning of economy. They know that the only way to get something done right is to do it yourself. They are up at the crack of dawn and go to roost at twilight so as not to waste electricity on lighting, although utility companies managed to convince several generations of farmers that keeping lights on in the henhouse all night would mean significantly more egg profit. All it meant was significantly more utility profit. The hens knew. They didn't ask for lights. They wanted a full night's sleep so they could live longer and healthier.

In thirty years without night lights, I have experienced exactly one sick hen, and have produced just about as many eggs per hen as the electric experts claim come from lighted coops—actually more because my hens enjoy two or three more years of productive life than public-utility hens.

The hen is a model of economy. She eats bugs and worms and weed seeds and grass and table scraps and half-digested grain in the cow manure. There is hardly anything she won't eat, in fact, except citrus. She will keep the barn free of accidentally spilled grain that would draw mice. She will even eat a mouse, if she can corner one. She will eat pests in the garden; heaven help the slug that she focuses her beady little eye on. Three hens can make their entire living off a medium-sized yard, plus table and garden scraps and maybe a handful of corn every day. All they need is water, and they can get that some of the time from dew, rain puddles, and snow. They are much easier to care for than a dog, and don't bark all night. In return, a trio of hens will provide a human family with an adequate annual supply of eggs.

The hen's chief form of entertainment is singing, and while she's no Streisand, her music is more soothing than rock and roll, and is so redolent with contentment as to supply the human listener with more consolation than a hundred-dollar-an-hour psychiatrist. She likes dust baths and will make for herself a suitable tub wherever she can find some dry dirt to wallow in, thereby protecting herself from lice. She goes to her coop dutifully as dark approaches, without any help from her human caretaker other than closing the door so foxes, raccoons, and coyotes don't get her. (Actually, she will roost in a tree if allowed to do so.) In her coop she becomes a recycler without peer, making better compost of her manure and bedding than a $100,000 mechanical compost-turner can do. She likes to scratch furiously in the bedding under her roost (sawdust from a carpentry shop makes good bedding, and dry leaves work okay, too). By this movement she mixes her droppings over and over again until the manure and the bedding become one earthy, granulated, dry, odorless compost that you can handle with your bare hands. Chicken manure compost is so fertile that it will increase the yields in your garden and decrease the size of the plot you need to grow the hens' corn.

And is her scratching just a nervous tic? No way. With knowledge no economist taught her, she scratches through the bedding, consuming tiny specks of litter that provide her with vitamins and minerals, especially vitamins B-12 and K. If you feed the eggshells back to her, she also gets the extra calcium needed to keep her future eggshells strong. As her final contribution to the economy, when she ceases to lay many eggs (at three to five years of age), she makes heavenly *coq au vin*, such as you can find only in famous French restaurants.

Nor do these examples sum up the whole of chicken economics. Andy Lee, who is an excellent representative of what the new garden economy is all about, has written a marvelous little book called *Chicken Tractor* (Good Earth Publications, 1994; available from Chelsea Green), in which he details how to use chickens in a small moveable pen to fertilize, cultivate, and control weeds and pests in garden plots. As the new garden economy gets established, forward progress in this kind of biological technology will accelerate.

Now, bear with me as I make the significant point. (After all, it took me fifty years to understand this.) A 3-chicken garden farm requires very little work, makes no negative demands on the environment, but adds to the ecological health of all. Assume that 100 million people in the U.S. (about two-fifths of our population) keep three chickens each. Add to that number another 10 million 30-chicken units (like mine) operated just like the 3-chicken one, only calling for two- to- five-acre homesteads. Then add to that 3 million more 100-chicken units operated like the smaller ones, only on ten- to twenty-acre homesteads. With a hundred hens, you can substitute labor for capital—even if you raise all of their grain (about an acre's worth) yourself—without any punishing physical work and with miniscule out-of-pocket costs. Unlike big agribusiness, you are not lashed to the stern world of finance: No payroll to meet, no interest on investment to pay, no stockbrokers to please; no fear of what the Chicago Board of Trade will do tomorrow, nor the berserk farm-policy politicians in Washington; not even, as we shall see, constant worry about weather.

I believe this adds up to 900 million chickens, or approximately 225 billion eggs per year (at a conservative estimate of 250 per hen per year) and an awful lot of *coq au vin* and chicken soup. In fact, half of those hens could be butchered young, as broilers, to provide every man, woman, and child in this country with nearly two fried chickens apiece, and there would still be more than enough eggs to go around.

If I calculate correctly, less than half of the American people, 113 million, would be involved in the production. Many folks aren't able to raise even three chickens, for various reasons, and many, I'm sure, could not be persuaded that doing so would be a pleasant, interesting hobby. These are the people the other half would sell their surplus eggs to. Most of the eggs would reach their consumers having never been inside a truck nor caused one pothole in the road.

But let us assume that my wild "what if" were toned down to a more "sensible" scenario where just one-fourth of the people raised chickens. Obviously, they could do so quite well with very small farms.

The significance of this distributive garden economy becomes clear when you compare it with the consolidated animal-factory economy we have currently embraced. About ten miles south of where I live, a large egg-manufacturing company called AgriGeneral is building a complex of factories, each unit of which will house 2.5 million hens in a cluster of buildings, with four or five such clusters planned within about a twenty-mile radius. Each 2.5-million-hen unit will require 40,000 bushels of corn and 420 tons of soybean meal *per week*. That's 2 million bushels of corn per year or, for 14 million hens, nearly 12 million bushels, quite a bit more than the 8.5-million-bushel output of our entire county. Experts calculate that 14 million hens produce about 84,000 tons of manure a year, as many as 2 million people do. Approximately 700 chickens per every 2.5 million will die each day from "natural" causes, based on historical averages in facilities such as this. (According to the National Humane Society, 9.4 million factory fowl nationwide died unnaturally in the heat wave of 1995.) And one of the egg factories that AgriGeneral's owner used to operate in Germany lost some 60 thousand hens to salmonella in 1994. He spent time in prison in Germany after conviction in 1996 on charges of inhumanity to both chickens and a worker who was trying to delouse the factory hens.

In a factory operation, all that grain must be hauled in and all that waste hauled out at an enormous cost in fuel, as well as truck and road maintenance. Each 2.5 million hens must support a payroll of about sixty workers. Control of odor and manure runoff become constant, extremely expensive problems. A plague of flies on the neighborhood has already been generated by the first 2.5-million unit in operation. Even when regulations are followed, eventually the manure must be hauled and spread farther and farther away to avoid overdosing the soil with nitrogen, phosphorus, and trace elements. More expense.

Two and a half million hens need 180,000 gallons of water per day plus 3,000 gallons per day for egg washing (the latter process necessitating a storage pond or tank, another potential pollution problem). In the case of AgriGeneral's new Ohio operation, all that water will come from wells. Neighbors fear that their shallow private wells will go dry. And they already say that their property values are declining because no one wants to live anywhere near the place. Worst of all perhaps, the chaos and strife in the community (between those who think they will profit from the huge factory farm and those who think they will be financially and environmentally harmed) have unleashed a hatred that will, I fear, never go away.

The payoff? After all costs are paid, commercial egg producers currently clear a couple of pennies per dozen eggs, and mammoth operations such as this one, with so many problems and such horrendous expenses, clear less than that. At this particular factory, labor troubles have escalated: workers who make only $5.50 per hour need to work long overtime hours at the same hourly rate, because a hen factory is still considered a farm by Ohio law and therefore isn't required to pay overtime. This practice is being challenged in court.

Nor is there any way to factor in the many, many hours that politicians and government agencies have spent trying to handle the problems and protests that this huge egg factory has generated. Those people make a lot more than $5.50 per hour.

And to what avail? Time and time again, people who eat our eggs tell us how much better they are than "boughten" eggs.

All these problems and all this gross expense would be avoided by a distributive economy of small chicken farms and gardens. My *cost* per dozen eggs is hardly a nickel. In fact, there might be only profit involved in my "operation" because if I weren't fiddling with these chickens, I would probably be out doing something that costs real money, like investing in ostriches.

It doesn't take a genius to begin to see that a garden economy might not be as preposterous as it at first sounds.

I'm a great believer in the pessimistic observation that humans collectively won't do the right thing unless the right thing also happens to be more pleasurable than the wrong thing or unless they have no other choice. I do not believe that suddenly even 50 percent of Americans are going to roll up their sleeves and start digging up the backyard with all the naive bravado of those poor deluded young communists in Russia marching off to work in factories in the 1940s. We are going to learn to do these things on a small scale because we won't have much choice in the matter. The alternative is not sustainable. Once the change is forced on us, people will realize that the new economy ain't so bad after all. As millions of gardeners now will tell you, horticulture and husbandry on a small scale are quite a bit more enjoyable and interesting than sitting in front of a computer screen for twelve hours a day, or standing at an assembly line for sixty hours a week, or circling O'Hare in an airplane for what seems like half your lifetime, all the while waiting for downsizing to take away your job.

Let us assume for a moment that the food and economic situation in the world is not as hunky-dory as agribusiness wants us to believe. Suppose that as more land is taken out of farming (at the rate of one acre every three minutes in the U.S. right now), as the population continues to rise, as disease racks the animal factories, and as the prices of tractor fuel and metal refining keep mounting, that factory-style fossil-fuel farming hits the wall. Then what?

Here's a happy alternative: the little red hen economy. About 70 million acres are planted to corn in the U.S. every year. What if 70 million people each planted one acre, as I do. Or 10 million grew seven acres, as could be done in the very low-tech manner I employ? Compare the costs of a homesteader's spare time, recreational labor, small and inexpensive tools, and land paid for as a part of the homeplace and lifestyle, to the enormous capital investment and overhead that the farm-industrialist must make. Add to this the taxpayer expense of an army of agricultural bureaucrats and "experts," along with all those farm subsidies; the production and transportation costs; the personal stress on the industrial farmer; and the enormous strain on the environment. How weird is my idea of a garden economy, really?

Technology has convinced society that food production must be a highly complex, expensive operation—when the truth lies in the opposite direction. In the October 1995 issue of *Rural New England* magazine, my favorite out-country periodical, editor Robert Kaldenbach tells a wonderful fable. A man decides to raise sheep but doesn't know how. Being a logical sort, he asks the sheep. They tell him all they really need is a bite of grass, a sip of water, and a pinch of salt. As long as the shepherd follows his flock's advice, things go well, but the man is not content, always wanting to do more for the sheep. He asks them if they need a barn, better kinds of grass, more hay, some grain, protection against wolves. To all of which the sheep answer that all they need is a bite of grass, a sip of water, and a pinch of salt. Nevertheless, the man drives himself into a frenzy of debt and stress providing all the things he thinks the sheep need, and complaining about all the trouble this has cost him. The sheep always respond by saying they only need a bite of grass, a sip of water, and a pinch of salt. At long last, the man has understood: he himself has been the cause of his problems, not the sheep. "Sheep don't need much, it is true," he finally admits. "Most of this is for me."

# CHAPTER 2

# WHAT IS A GARDEN?

The gardener defines the garden. Each of us in the act of gardening expresses what that activity means to us, and so gardens are as different one from another as humans are. Donnie Downs in Columbus, Ohio, without space for a "real" garden in his present circumstances, raises tomatoes and pole beans in big patio pots, on trellises he brazed together from copper tubing. The trellises have an artfulness about them as metal sculpture that is interesting (well, maybe "startling" would be a better word) to look at, even in winter when they are not draped with bean or tomato vines.

Charles MacArthur of Sangerville, Maine, on the other hand, considers his entire eighty acres of wild hay, for which he swapped a fishing pier on the coast, to be an experimental garden where he nourishes to fruition his ecological inventiveness. No freer spirit lives in Maine, I have a notion. He once sent me a picture of himself giving balloon rides at a nudist resort. Among many other pursuits, he sells gallon jugs of liquid chicken manure that he labels "Chicken Chic—Smells like hell and works like the devil." Chic? "Well that's about as close as you can come without actually saying it," he says wryly. He has raised cucumbers and lettuce in thirty-below-zero weather in a plastic greenhouse warmed by hot water. The water is heated by acting as a coolant for a unique waste-to-energy gasification "reclaimer" that he invented to burn trash without pollution. He also tells me, with a roguish smile, that hot water (practically a free by-product of his reclaimer) kills grass and weeds with less risk to the environment than herbicides. He plants mostly trees on his eighty-acre hay garden, experimenting with fast-growing species like paulownia. He intends the wood to eventually become fuel for heating homes and, indirectly, a source of methane gas for various purposes including running his old John Deere tractor.

John McMahan is a free spirit too, but of a different mold. His orchard in southern Indiana is a naturalized planting of mulberry and persimmon trees that he never prunes, never sprays, never does much of anything to. Simply harvests the fruit, as do the birds and wild animals. Mulberry muffins taste just like blueberry muffins, he says, and while the birds are eating the surplus fruit, they are not eating his cherries, strawberries, and raspberries. When I visited him, he gave me a taste of persimmon pudding made from his grandmother's recipe (see his self-published book *Farmer John Outdoors,* published by CompuArt Designs, Columbus, Indiana, 1995). As he claimed, it was just as delicious as desserts made with more mainstream fruits. Persimmons, even wild native ones, also make a unique and unusually flavorful ice cream.

My grandfather kept what he called a strawstack melon garden. To grow melons, he would put a fence around the spot where the winter strawstack had stood. All that remained in spring would be about a foot of straw and manure trampled flat by the livestock. He would plant melon seeds in that mulch when the weather warmed up. Towards autumn, he would come back to gather the melons: No weeding, no spraying, no work at all, except cutting up the melons into slivers a kid could handle.

Jan Dawson and Andy Reinhart, near Bellefontaine, Ohio, maintain a gourd-and-flower garden, along with large plots of vegetables. They sell unusual gourds, especially long-necked ones, which they bend and twist into dramatically exotic (some even rather erotic) shapes before curing. But their main business, from which they make most of their living, is selling dried-flower arrangements using the plants and flowers they grow. They trim and bunch and dry them in a special barn they built at the garden's edge. They sell mostly at the farmer's market in Columbus, Ohio. Next to the garden is their modest, partially in-ground home, heated with a wood-burning stove and fuel from their woodlot. Neither Jan nor Andy has an outside job anymore, and together they have been able to make enough money from their garden enterprises to finance their frugal lifestyle. "We saved our money from other jobs until we could own our place here free and clear," says Jan. "This is both our living and our recreation, so we don't have to spend much money." Adds Andy, "I'm an individualist with some different views of life from most people. But saying that reminds me of my favorite bumper sticker: 'Individualists unite.' I appreciate the irony of that slogan. I've learned that it is very helpful in practical and spiritual ways to unite with others who share my 'different' views."

For naturalist Miriam Rothschild, butterflies were the focus of her gardening, and she grew whatever plants lured these winged jewels (see her delightful 1983 book *The Butterfly Garden,* written with Clive Farrell and published by Michael Joseph/Rainbird, London, 1983). Interestingly, although she was recognized widely for her work in parasitology, and published valuable papers on esoteric subjects such as gigantism in winkles, the behavior of seagulls, the defensive poisons of moths and butterflies (I'm reading from the jacket of her book), and the life cycle of intestinal worms, she was "educated at home, took no public examinations, and holds no university degrees." I mention this as another example of why I tell young people to avoid college whenever possible and get to work doing what they like to do.

Robert Kaldenbach might define his very contrary gardening efforts as the seedbed out of which grew his *Rural New England* magazine, my current favorite among country publications. It radiates the humor, honesty, and practicality that can only come from real experience in a garden economy. "We have tried and failed to launch a 500-bird free-range flock of hens, and we have tried and succeeded any number of times to raise a 6-bird backyard flock," he writes in the August 1995 issue. "Even college professors can master the skills required to construct a chickenhouse . . . Those who previously thought the hammer and sickle merely archaic flag illustrations will find they can actually learn to use both these tools . . . Computer programmers and freelance writers will find their complexion clearing, new muscle tone, hearty appetite and a fresh outlook on life's prospects once they have built something that stands . . . Poultry, poultry is the way."

On another occasion (July 1995) he reviews a ho-hum how-to book for homesteaders with these words: "Here we find 128 pages of generality. If you don't already know everything here, your wife shouldn't allow you to wander from her side at the county fair. This is a clipboard full of check lists impersonating as a book, a dreary lifeless recital of Everyman's Home Companion. It will find two uses: (1) as a gift to the League of Women Voters Annual Book Sale, and (2) as a doorstop. Make that just one use, it's too light to hold open the screen door."

Mary Butters, a longtime active environmentalist in her home country in Idaho, was kind enough to write to me and tell me what she was doing these days. She could say that her 5-acre garden's main crop is the organic foods mail-order business that grew out of it. She carved her garden out of her husband's 650-acre commercial farm. (How's that for being contrary?) Her original purpose was to find products that farmers in her area could grow organically so as to stop the annual chemical drenching of farmland. (I can imagine how that went over in the local community. Her husband probably had to quit going to the coffee shop with the other farmers.) She grows beans, grains, vegetables, herbs, and spices—all certified organic—and sells them through her Paradise Farm catalog. Though she and her husband and children use a computer and a fax machine in the business, they also use a wood-burning stove and an outhouse in their daily living. As an example of how potent a garden economy can be, Mary refused a big company's multimillion dollar offer for her business. "I'm a person of passion and values," she says. "My soul would be gone if I sold out."

Down the road from us, Ann and Brad Billock keep a tiny but wondrously productive mulch garden, if ever that word applies. They rotary-till only to prepare seedbeds. Shortly after plants are up and the soil is warm, they cover the space between the rows and between the plants in each row with decaying leaves that they get from our village composting site. Their vegetable garden is neat, above all other features, and is laid out as if with a ruler into four plots, each approximately twenty by twenty-five feet in size. Canning and freezing what they don't eat fresh, keeping a few hens, and feeding out two beef steers per year (one to sell to pay the cost of feeding both), they rarely buy food staples. "Almost everyone lays out too big a garden," Ann remarks, rolling her eyes significantly at my gardens, which wander all over an acre.

Dutch Zimmerman, a close friend who recently passed away, combined gardening with running a gas station in our village. Actually, he owned two different stations, moving from one to the other in midlife, but neither one was more than four blocks from his beloved rose garden. Roses and garage work might seem like a strange combination, and it truly was for Dutch. Pumping gas he didn't mind. Even changing tires was not so bad. But he hated working on car motors, and would swear steadily whenever he had to do it, while I stood by and giggled at him. "Why would a man who hates cars own a gas station?" I asked him once. "The same reason you write books but hate editors," he answered drily.

Dutch's garden, like his service station, was a model of neatness. He grew many kinds of vegetables and fruits, but his real love was the roses. He would come home from cursing cars to prune and weed some one hundred varieties of roses, all of which he could name correctly, all set out in straight rows like marching soldiers. In the fall, he enclosed each plant with a bit of 12-inch-high chicken wire, which he stuffed full of leaves and grass clippings to protect the plants from winterkill. "And I spray the hell out of them," he said on my first visit to his inner sanctum, challenging me to make some organic protest. He relished showing me the stash of chemicals he had stored away, pointing out proudly that some of the ones that were now outlawed, he could still use regularly.

Lloyd Riggle's outlook on life is vastly different than Dutch's, but Lloyd is a mechanic too (a genius at it, in my estimation). Yet the garden is the center of his and wife Dorothy's lives—so much so that Lloyd gave up his starring role at International Harvester, where he travelled the country solving mechanical problems no one else could handle, and retreated to a rural haven far from the madding crowd to live literally in his garden. His automotive repair shop, like his house, is positioned so close to the garden as to be part of it. He can go from work to play in ten seconds, and often does. He and Dorothy are very health-conscious, which is one reason they raise almost all the food they eat. The one thing they don't raise is corn for meal, which is how we got to know one another. I needed someone who could understand the mysteries of an old tractor, and Lloyd said that my open-pollinated corn made the best cornmeal he had ever eaten. That kind of trade is the beginning of real community.

Year in and year out, the Riggle garden outshines all the others in our neighborhood; makes no difference if the year is wet or dry, cold or hot. Yet they use no chemical fertilizers or sprays. They maintain big heaps of compost, turned by tractor front-end loader, to which they add and remove material continually. Every fall, they sow the whole garden to wheat, which they plow under in the spring for green manure. From the grove of trees around the buildings and gardens, they cut enough wood to heat their modest home. They also make their own soap, and can, freeze, and dry foods they don't eat fresh. Yet in none of their work do they need to exert themselves too much, because Lloyd has a power tool for every job, and if not, he will make one. I would venture to say that although the Riggles' yearly cash outlays for living expenses are less than those of the poorest family in the county, they live better, by contrary gardener standards, than the richest family in the county.

Cathrine Sneed has astounded the California penal system by proving that gardening can heal the troubled souls of prisoners, and often keeps them from becoming repeat offenders. She gave one of the most eloquent speeches I have ever read, one that she gave at the Fifteenth Annual E. F. Schumacher Lectures in October 1995. Cathrine was kind enough to send me her text and allow me to quote from it. The speech is a short history of the seventeen years during which she used her vision of "gardens everywhere" both to keep prisoners from becoming repeat offenders and to turn people who were headed toward jail toward a more self-respecting lifestyle. You can also read about Cathrine's work with inmates in Patricia Hynes's book *A Patch of Eden: America's Inner-City Gardeners* (Chelsea Green, 1996).

As a law student, she went to work in the sheriff's department at the San Francisco County jail. She became completely frustrated by her failure to rehabilitate prisoners. The pathetic hopelessness of the situation so depressed her that she ended up in the hospital—"going in and out for almost a year . . . I wasn't getting any better. My doctor said, 'Well you're not responding . . . so you can go home and die or you can stay here and die.'"

But that very day a friend gave her a copy of Steinbeck's *The Grapes of Wrath*. "In it I found a powerful message: hope lies in the land, and if people who are feeling hopeless can connect to the land, and stay connected, then they will be okay."

The thought struck her that she could rehabilitate criminals through gardening. She hopped out of bed and asked to be released from the hospital. Soon she was back working with the prisoners, starting her "Garden Project." She was still so weak that the prisoners had to carry her to and from the old farm she had located for a garden. She found out later that the sheriff deputies had been making bets on whether the prisoners would rape her or just beat her up.

"For ten years, we concentrated on making the program at the jail work," says Cathrine. "During that time, I saw tremendous change in thousands of prisoners. But what began to worry me was what happened to them when they got out of jail. They were going right back into the environment that had put them in jail. They had no choice." This situation led to the second major part of her work: a garden where ex-cons and their families could come to work, sell vegetables, and earn a little money. "For many of these people, jail was better than home," she says. She learned about a vacant lot, covered with garbage that might make a half-acre garden. Pressed for cash, she asked the owner to just write her a check for bus money so the ex-cons could get to the site. "He pointed to the empty garbage lot and he said something I wouldn't have thought of: 'Grow something and I'll buy what you grow. Then you'll have the money.'"

So the ex-cons cleared the lot and started growing vegetables. Around 125 people worked there in the summer of 1995, and 600 all told since 1991. "That meant that every head of lettuce got stroked quite a bit," says Cathrine. "There was absolutely no weeds, mountains of compost, and probably the most pampered spinach you'll ever meet." She recalled a young man who had been selling crack before, now picking and arranging spinach in the packing box with slow and satisfied care, too slow really for efficient work. "But at the same time I realized . . . that this young man knew he was producing something that was valuable, that looked beautiful, that was going somewhere, and some money was going to come back in return. He knew he was beginning to make himself and his family self-sufficient."

Cathrine went on to philosophize in words that, to me, ring with the angry hope of all contrary gardeners: "I suggest a sequel to Schumacher's book. Small is not only beautiful *but necessary.* I say that because I don't have thousands and thousands of dollars. I don't have a fancy office in a fancy place and a great big area to grow enough produce to supply the restaurants that want our food. What I do have is a lot of people who say, 'I want a chance; I want to work. I want to work *here.*' The idea that there isn't enough work for people, or the other idea that the kind of people I'm working with don't want to work, is just plain wrong."

For Skip Stauffer, a garden means mostly the beautiful and marvelous acreage of commercial herb gardens that surround her quaint home near Ada, Ohio. Her garden is her entrance back into the 19th century, in which she tries to live her life. I haven't visited her since 1986, but mutual acquaintances say she is still living as she did then, that is, as if today were a hundred years ago.

She was wearing forgotten clothes the day I stopped by: a long, homespun (literally homespun) peasant frock, with a ruffled petticoat peeking out from underneath it. Over her frock and a long-sleeved blouse, she wore a full-length white apron splotched with tomato juice from the tomatoes she was canning. She was barefoot. Except for the absence of the high-button shoes she wears in cooler weather, this was the way Skip Stauffer dressed every day. Her heart was a hundred years old.

In the backyard, next to the summer kitchen, stood a homemade food-dryer about the size of a refrigerator, with several shelves inside and a tiny woodstove at the bottom. She dried much of her fruit and vegetable crop in there, as people used to before refrigeration. The amount of fuel needed to fire the stove for drying was very minimal, she pointed out. (What a way to get rid of the scores of duplicate and unnecessary catalogs that besiege us!) Mick, her husband, built the dryer. Skip envisaged the 19th century, and Mick rendered it in wood and metal.

Next to the dryer, a pot hung from a tripod with a pile of kindling under it, ready to be fired. Here Skip cooked much of the food her family ate in the summertime. She kept a goat in the pasture for milk. There used to be sheep, too, providing the wool from which she spun yarn and wove fabric. Now she bought her raw wool from a nearby shepherd.

A gray arctic fox pup, half grown, was tethered to a chair in the yard. The pup whined for attention. Skip picked it up as if it were a baby. Its jaw widened frighteningly around her chin, but the teeth did not bite. Cradling the pup, she led me through the herb gardens, as she did many visitors, many times a year. In the pond nearby, ducks and geese floated, and a wild green heron stood on one leg, studying the passing hours.

But it was when I stepped into the tree-shrouded house in the center of the gardens—past the giant basket made of grapevines on the porch; past the broom made of twigs; past the doors with handles of curved, weathered pieces of tree branch—that I began to grasp the true spirit of the place. I had to pause at the door for my eyes to grow accustomed to the dark interior. There was no overhead electric illumination to switch on, only kerosene lamps to light. A small skylight sent a piercing sunbeam down onto a braid of red onions and several bunches of herbs drying on the wall. Another skylight illuminated the sink, where a child was peeling tomatoes. As my eyes began to know the dark room, I found myself standing in the middle of an early American kitchen. I was struck with an impulse to sit down and be quiet, as if I had just sauntered into an empty church. Skip lit candles. "Yes, I hand-dip the candles myself and, no, they aren't scented. I don't scent my soap either. Housewives a hundred years ago didn't have time for that, and neither do I." She grinned, looking at the candles. "Eating by candlelight is romantic even if you're only having pea soup."

A room off the kitchen, on a lower level, she called "the but'try" in the old-fashioned way. Here she stored lidded jars of dried fruits, canned goods, baskets of potatoes, and wooden bins of flour and meal that a commercial mill ground for her, as much as a hundred pounds at a time.

The pie safe held leftover baked goods. "But not any leftover pies," she said. "My pies don't last that long."

The house was not without electricity, but what there was, was used sparingly. A tiny bulb stayed lit in the far corner of the kitchen to cast a dim glow upon the darkest recesses of shelves and drawers. Somewhere, hidden from view, were a deep freezer, a refrigerator, and a washer. "If it were just me, I'd live totally in the past," said Skip. "But the kids have had to make enough adjustments as it is. They have a television upstairs. They wear the same kind of clothes their friends do. We have a modern bathroom, but Mick built a wooden seat around and over the toilet bowl so it would look like an outhouse."

"You can actually live quite well and cheaply using more past technology and less modern technology," she said. She believed that the influence of her grandparents had generated her fascination with an earlier America. "My father was a successful businessman in Detroit, and neither he nor Mother were much interested in the rural life of their parents. We had the nice house in suburbia, the maid, the whole bit. But I lived for our visits to Grandfather's farm. I just became totally taken up with the culture that produced his way of life, and resolved at an early age to live as much like that as I could."

The only worker who did not move at a hustling pace on Primitive Acres, as Skip called her gardens, was the scarecrow facing the road in the front gardens. It was dressed in a bonnet and smock that any 19th century gardener would have been proud to wear. Skip spent about as much time in the gardens as the scarecrow. "I'm out here whenever I'm not doing something else," she said. Then she laughed. "One day, I was hoeing when a neighbor pulled up along the road in his pickup and stopped. 'I've got to tell you what I did, though it's kind of embarrassing,' he told me. 'When I drove by earlier, I waved at your scarecrow.'"

Anna and Harlan Hubbard passed away recently, but they remain the best examples of contrary gardening that I know about personally. Surrounded by their gardens and sixty acres of woodland, their house stood along the Ohio River, inaccessible by car and shut off from electricity. When I walked down the rough horse-road through the woods to visit them nearly twenty years ago, I feared that I might find two darlings of the richer class playing a game, or two wild visionaries living in squalor and disarray. But what I found was a place of order and discipline, and a lifestyle of economy and serenity. The Hubbards were far from rich in terms of income, but wealthy beyond measure in the art of living. A Steinway grand piano dominated one of the two rooms in the little house they had built. Anna played the piano, Harlan the violin, and both were accomplished musicians. They read much and widely, often aloud to each other, in German and French as well as English. They rowed across the Ohio to get to the library at Madison, Indiana every month. Harlan was also an accomplished artist in oils and watercolors, and what meager cash income they earned came from occasionally selling a painting, plus rent from a house they owned in town (and which Harlan had also built).

Without electricity or gas power, the Hubbards lived elegantly, because they had understood from the start that the skills of contrary gardening required as much study, experience, and aptitude as learning to play a musical instrument well, paint a picture artfully, or build a good house. They did not go blindly to the garden and the tree grove and the barn; they first spent years mastering the craft of subsistence living. Before formally beginning to practice this most demanding but comforting of arts, they served an internship in contrary gardening by floating down the Ohio and Mississippi Rivers in a shantyboat, living off the river and the passing shoreline for a year.

Several times while I was visiting the Hubbards, Harlan emphasized how the garden was the central and key factor in his and Anna's existence, essential both for physical sustenance and for the vital spiritual sustenance of being free from the slavery of a salaried work schedule, and thus able to order their lives to their own priorities. He referred to this second advantage as generating a "blissful exuberance in my soul."

On the early April day I visited the Hubbards, Harlan was working in the early garden, on a hillside shelf above the flood line of the river. He did not plant a lower garden on the richer, narrow creek-bottom till late, when dangers of spring flooding had passed. In the higher garden, he had built his cold frames, and in them I noticed, much to my surprise, about thirty little pots of peas, already three inches tall. When I remarked that not many people started peas in frames, he explained that the moles in his rich, heavily mulched gardens had become so numerous that they would attack the sprouting peas in early spring. By starting the peas in a cold frame, the sides of which were sunk fifteen inches into the soil, he avoided the moles until the plants were growing well. Then he could transplant the peas to the garden proper, by which time the moles were no longer interested. Transplanting the fairly large number of pea plants necessary to get an appreciable early crop was not that much of a job either, because he found that three or four plants to a pot did just as well as one.

Watching Harlan wield a heavy, wide-bladed planter hoe was an edification in itself. His soft, loamy soil seemed to suck in the hoe blade without effort from him. He needed only to rock slightly backward as the hoe settled into the ground and pull the sunken blade easily toward him to achieve a surprisingly broad furrowing of the soil surface. In just a few strokes, he had readied a ten- by fifteen-foot bed for planting, as fast as I could have done it with a motorized tiller.

Economy of muscular movement was apparent in all of Harlan's work, especially cutting the wood that served as the couple's only source of fuel for heat and cooking. Most of the wood for constructing the house had also come from his woodlot. "The reason the ceiling joists are sapling sycamore is because those were the straightest logs in the woods," Harlan said with a smile. The floor boards were of sycamore too, because the grain won't rise or splinter (which is why this is also the wood of choice for butcher blocks). At work in the woods, Harlan swung the ax effortlessly, yet one whack sheared a two-inch branch from the log, and two whacks severed three-inch limbs. Sawing logs, he rocked gently at one end of a one-man crosscut, and the blade bit through an eight-inch log almost as fast as a chainsaw would. The same smooth flow of muscle was noticeable as he cranked his little grain mill to make bread flour. His body seemed to coil and then uncoil like a spring around the crank, and the meal streamed steadily from the burrs. Dipping pails of water from the cistern and carrying them, two at a time, on the shoulder yoke he had made, strength and suppleness moved in cadence with the laws of gravity and of leverage. At this level of muscular harmony, physical labor became not work so much as sport, as satisfying as making a perfect hook-slide into second base. All the more impressively, Harlan was over seventy years old.

The Hubbards grew a complete garden-catalog list of fruits and vegetables, and also betook themselves of many wild foods. But not all their work was utilitarian. As we walked along surveying his food plants, many species of birds distracted Harlan from our conversation, and he would pause and watch each one with great pleasure. "What we do here draws all kinds of birds," he said. "Bird-watching is probably our favorite pastime." It was nevertheless difficult for me to keep my eye on the birds, because of the array of wild blue larkspur that adorned the whole mountainside. Here was flower gardening that required no work at all—that required *not* working, in fact. "The larkspur will disappear," Harlan said, "if the hillsides are cleared for pasture or grass."

Next to the rhubarb and comfrey was a patch of day lilies just emerging from the soil. Harlan cut a day lily shoot and offered it to me. It was delicious, as he promised. He dug a Jerusalem artichoke root, something I never cared for before, and cut a slice to show me how crisp and sweet it tasted after winter and before it started to grow again. He mentioned that the nettles were not ready yet. "Cream of nettle soup is a favorite of mine," he said. He and Anna relied on wild raspberries and blackberries rather than tame ones. Again, no work was involved except harvesting, and, said Anna, the taste was better. Elderberries came from the woods' edge too, and Anna preserved them to eat with spring rhubarb. "Elderberries and rhubarb make each other taste better," she said. "So do gooseberries and rhubarb." The gooseberry patch was treated as a wild fruit, that is, allowed to spread as it naturally does, into a sunny glade in the woods. Again, no work except harvesting.

As much as the wild lands around them, the river supplied the couple with a steady supply of food. They put out and tended a trotline between floodtime and freeze-up, as provisioning required. In earlier years, they had traded catfish to neighbors for milk, butter, and meat, but now they kept a little herd of goats for their use. The goats also helped with weed control in the garden. When a plot was rotated out of vegetables, it was allowed to grow up in weeds temporarily and Harlan cut them for the goats, or allowed the goats to graze them. If there were weeds to pull in growing gardens, these were fed to the goats also. In return, the goat manure went back on the garden, completing the symbiosis between husbandry and botany that is so essential to the best contrary gardening. "Goats relish weeds more than pasture, actually," said Harlan.

The goat barn stood about a hundred feet from the upper garden. By deploying homemade fences made of tree branches around growing crops, Harlan could allow the goats to have the run of the homestead, more or less, keeping brush from taking over around the house. There was no lawnmower.

Harlan showed me his sunken 55-gallon barrels, in which he kept potatoes, beets and other root crops through the winter. He had made slanted lids to carry off rain, with little ventilating windows covered with hardware cloth on each side of the lid. When I got home, I immediately installed two such barrels next to our garden, and have used them as food-storage pits without problems ever since.

The Hubbards also used two steel barrels (which had come their way as flotsam on the river) to make a cheap but effective meat and fish smoker. One barrel was dug into a steep hillside horizontally, with the open end facing out. Then, twenty feet or so higher up the hill, a second barrel stood vertically, the upward-facing end open except for a piece of tin loosely covering it. Regular drainage tile (any kind of 4-inch piping would work, I presume) connected the back of the horizontal lower barrel to the bottom of the vertical upper barrel. A very small, smoldering hickory fire in the lower barrel could then generate all the smoke necessary to travel up the pipe and into the upper barrel, where meat or fish was hung to be smoked. At this point, the smoke was cool enough to cure the food without cooking it. I came home and built the same arrangement, and it has worked satisfactorily for us ever since. The smoker works because it is an extremely simple setup, as is the food-storage pit.

Through their elegant simplicity, the Hubbards were able to treat me to a meal that might be the envy of the most extravagant restaurant-goer in Paris. Anna served a salad containing sliced, fresh Jerusalem artichokes; fresh violets, including the blossoms; parsley that had survived the winter; new Bibb lettuce from the cold frame; and day lily shoots. This was garnished lightly with oil and raspberry-flavored vinegar, all sprinkled over with crumbled black walnut meats. The soup was made from goat meat stock, canned in a previous year and possessing superb flavor. The main dish was smoked chevon, shredded and creamed and flanked by fresh asparagus. The heavy, moist homemade bread was blended from flour, half whole-wheat and half soybean. Fresh rhubarb pie followed with sweet, fresh, untainted goat's milk and a choice of comfrey or sassafras tea.

During my visit, I had to be content with a privy for a bathroom, but that proved to be a pleasant interlude, too. As I sat there, I became aware of a wren in a nest on the wall beside me. Mother Wren stared at me, but did not move. I felt that I should talk to her, but could think of nothing that might interest a wren. There was little odor in the privy, since waste dropped about ten feet below into a tub (the outhouse having been built on the side of a steep incline). A pipe under the toilet seat vented odors away through the wall, and all that was necessary, after use, was to take two coal-shovel scoops of ashes from a nearby bucket and drop them down the hole. Twice a week, Harlan lifted the tub below onto his wheelbarrow and hauled it to a windrow of compost in the woods. The pile kept moving, he explained, because he was constantly adding all kinds of organic waste to one end while removing finished compost from the other end. He had to curve the windrow into a semi-circle, or eventually he would have had to push the wheelbarrow halfway across his property. Before replacing the tub below the privy, he put an inch-deep layer of finished compost in the tub. "The microorganisms in it will get the composting process started quicker that way," he said.

I asked Harlan why he didn't write a book that would explain every last detail of how he and Anna did everything. "Oh, that would be too tedious," he said. "No publisher would publish it and few people would read it."

He kept insisting, however, that the work itself was neither tedious nor boring nor backbreaking, but easier physically as well as mentally, in fact, than what most other people had to do to make a living. He said it best in his book, *Payne Hollow* (The Eakins Press, 1974):

> . . . I try to conceive a life of more leisure, a condition which men have ever been trying to achieve by various means—by forcing slaves or captives in war to do the menial work, or by letting it devolve upon women-folk, or by hiring servants, and nowadays by innumerable machines and gadgets. This last solution allows everyone to play the master, but it is well known that machines are in a way to become masters of men . . . We get all our living by as direct means as possible, that we may be self-sufficient and avoid contributing to the ruthless mechanical system that is destroying the earth . . . In this endeavor, no sacrifice is called for, no struggle or effort of will. Such a way is natural. Rather than hardship, it brings peace and inner rewards beyond measure.

Obviously, as many gardeners as there are, as many kinds of gardens there will be. But a few generalities may be in order if they are not pressed too hard on reality:

- *Contrary gardeners order their lives* so as to pursue their other career or job close to their gardens. This may not be true during one's entire life, but it nearly always becomes so eventually. I spent two hours commuting to and from work in Philadelphia every weekday for nine years, and I still gardened extensively. But I knew I could not and would not continue that madness. I knew I would eventually bring my work world close to my garden, even if it meant giving up a good job for whatever I could find nearby. The garden was my real career.
- *Contrary gardening is wholistic,* that is, it embraces the diversity of the whole food chain. Husbandry, even if involving only earthworms or the birds that the garden attracts, is as important as the plant-growing side of the operation, and is the means by which the greatest economy and pleasure are achieved. Likewise,

lawns and tree groves become a functional and functioning part of the garden.

- *Contrary gardening is rather pagan* in the original meaning of that word: *paganus* means "country dweller" in Latin. Those *pagani* of ancient Roman times were not interested in giving up their good life for anyone's idea of institutional religion or institutional politics or institutional economics. So the word *paganus* gradually took on a negative meaning among the institutional powermongers of the world. They couldn't control pagans, so pagans must be bad.

  Like the *pagani,* contrary gardeners today are motivated by a great love for the pleasures of eating good food and enjoying other physical stimulations of the natural and garden environment. Accompanied by the enforcing moderation of having to provide them by one's own hard work, these pleasures lead to a healthy spirituality of lovingness for all the natural universe, and a suspicion of any human effort to exploit nature for money. This love grows stronger as time passes, so that eventually, the garden becomes essential to the gardener's notion of quality living. He or she does not need to search fruitlessly for other paradises.

- *Inevitably, contrary gardeners want to share* the tremendous enjoyment they get from nurturing animals, plants, and themselves, and they will be tempted to start some sort of business selling their surplus garden food or some "value-added" product like wine or cheese or pastry or pasta. For some gardeners, this venture turns into a disaster, but for a few, it is the beginning of successful little food businesses that reward the society that fosters them, even if the businesspeople are "pagans."

There is much more reward waiting to be achieved. We could make of the earth a garden of Eden, but greed blinds us from understanding this. Go figure, Adam and Eve.

# CHAPTER 3

# GARDENING TO SAVE US FROM "THE ECONOMY"

I suppose I should have titled this chapter "Garden Accounting," but no one would have read it then. What I am referring to is not garden accounting in the usual sense anyway. I'm not talking about how you can save money by raising your own food, although this is important, especially if you have to try to live off of your Social Security. Nor am I going to dwell on how you can save even more money by becoming so delightfully absorbed in gardening that you forget about expensive pastimes, such as discoursing on the world's salvation in your favorite tavern or church. Nor am I going to describe how a garden can be a stepping-stone to profitable truck farming or subscription food marketing. Going into a gardening business may be a good idea for entrepreneurial types, especially if you have been downsized out of a job, but for most gardeners in love with privacy, it can prove to be a disaster.

What I am talking about here is quite the opposite. I am talking about how in gardening you can remove yourself from the enslaving dictums of financial accounting almost altogether. You do not have to worry about whether your work makes money in the usual sense. Your garden exists in a lovely place outside the hot arena of profit and loss, and this can be the beginning of true economy.

As a "nonprofit" gardener, you can help the economy at large, contradictory as this statement sounds. Surely, everyone agrees that some kind of economic reform is necessary when the world's richest country is the world's biggest debtor nation. The economists talk about an increase in jobs, but we are borrowing to get them, and mostly they are temporary or low-paying jobs. Both liberals and conservatives are in more agreement than usual that there has been a decline in the actual buying power and income of even middle-class people, while a small portion of those at the top of the money chain grow richer and a big bunch at the bottom grow poorer. What these poorer ones, and even lower-middle-class people, are going to live on in their old age is beyond me, even with the help of measly bucks from Social Security, as medical and housing costs rise. A garden economy offers a partial answer to this kind of economic worry.

There is a particular reason why gardening can become an antidote for the instability of "the economy." World grain stocks declined for three years prior to 1997 (news that was more or less suppressed until recently). No one can say for sure if this was a temporary dip or an omen of things to come.

Agribusiness thinks that the situation was only temporary, and that supplies will be back to "normal" in 1997. But even if this turns out to be true, world demand for food continues to soar. China just became a net importer of grain, once again. To help reverse the decline in grain stocks, U.S. farmers are being allowed to take erosive land out of the Conservation Reserve Program and plant it to grain. And in South America, there has already been an increase in the pace of clearing the rain forests, as agribusiness there foresees making a killing on possibly high future grain prices. Such "remedies" for sagging grain production could be suicidal in the long run. What if we have reached the time, long predicted by Les Brown of the Worldwatch Institute, when world population continues to rise while world grain production, as conventionally practiced by agribusiness, levels off?

Whatever your income, if you have even the smallest plot of ground, you can help head off such a catastrophe. Consider these ten points:

1. If managed properly, a half-acre yard can raise most of the food for two or three families.
2. You don't have to borrow money to start this kind of garden.
3. You don't have to meet a payroll to maintain it.

4. You don't have to worry about hitting the top of the market with your production. Every day is the top of the market for you.

5. If you save seed, use mostly hand tools, and recycle composted leaves and other wastes for fertility, you can garden with only miniscule expense.

6. You don't have to worry, as commercial farmers must, about how the government will screw up the market in an effort to control it.

7. You don't have to worry about competitors driving you out of business, nor do you have to worry about driving someone else out of business.

8. You don't have to worry about inflationary price rises in food or inputs. All inflation does is raise the value of your own time in your garden.

9. You don't have to worry about the environmental cost of gardening. In the very act of gardening, you sustain the environment.

10. You don't have to worry about fossil-fuel or food shortages in case of political or economic collapse. If even one-third of our 250 million Americans gardened seriously, there could be no such collapse.

The world of finance beyond our gardens is a grim place these days, and getting grimmer. We have never been able to achieve economic stability within our present economic system. Expansion is always required to keep up with exponential increases in money interest, which fuel inflation. "The economy" lurches from recession to inflation and back again. Consolidation of businesses and downsizing generate a constant dislocation of workers. Not all the wise ones of the Federal Reserve seem able to prevent this constant unrest, the fallout from which is a growing class of poor people. The old fundamentalist economists' belief in some "invisible hand," making sure the marketplace remains fair and balanced, is little more than a modern religious superstition, as ludicrous as believing in a thunderbolt-hurling Zeus.

Economic "invisible hands" continue to force people not only from the land, but from owning a house that has enough land with it for an ample garden, and even, in many cases, from owning a house at all. So, with no other way to provide some of their own food, clothing, and shelter, working people become more and more desperate for jobs. Job desperation scares them into becoming almost crazy for money, since this appears to be their only recourse. A sort of craven bitterness develops in people without a chance for a good job, and they become deceitful in public and cruel in private, very much like what happened to working people in England when the Industrial Revolution made them destitute, and forced them to work in factories under cruel and exploitive managers. The alternative of heading off into the frontier with a cow and an ax no longer exists; the frontiers are all covered with Coke cans. But the other alternative to regaining some portion of independence, and therefore self-esteem, remains: the garden.

The best way to see how gardeners help to alleviate the situation is to study the so-called gross domestic product, or GDP. The GDP is the total sum of money that changes hands in financial transactions, usually reckoned on a yearly basis. The world of finance and the world of government interpret this figure as a measurement of economic growth.

But many money transactions have nothing to do with healthy economic growth and might be very unhealthy investments, while other nonmonetary transactions are vital to the economy but ignored by the GDP. For example, included in the GDP are the monies spent on the Gulf War. How did that contribute to healthy growth? A hefty contributor to the GDP was the recent O. J. Simpson trial. How did that contribute to healthy growth? How do the millions of GDP dollars spent on gambling contribute to healthy growth?

Not calculated into the GDP are the uncountable billions of dollars that are saved when people and businesses operate in ways that sustain environmental health. Even more outrageous, the billions of dollars worth of environmental destruction that occur to make the GDP look good are not calculated into the debit side of the GDP.

Also not counted are the endless millions of private actions that do not involve cash outlays. Thousands of grandparents take care of grandchildren for free so the mothers and fathers can both work to keep the

GDP rolling along. Millions of other parents stay home and take care of their children themselves. Some families home-school their children, saving the public school system huge sums of money. Some people build their own homes in their spare time, do volunteer work, help take care of the sick and dying who can't afford hospitals or retirement homes—all for no money. Without their uncounted contributions, so much more tax and insurance money would have to be paid out that it would break both the government and the insurance companies.

Some forty million gardeners and garden farmers operate food production systems outside the world of the GDP. Their food is not properly counted in the GDP, nor are the many advantages of a gardening way of life upon which the economy depends, such as stable families and communities, knowledgeable sensitivity about environmental issues, and the inculcation of virtues without which chaos would reign.

It seems to me that the part of "the economy" that depends on biological processes, not industrial processes—especially food, but also renewable resources such as cotton and wool and other natural fibers for clothing, and wood for construction, furniture, and fuel—is particularly vulnerable to the volatile and chaotic conditions of the industrial manufacturing marketplace. An ear of corn grows at its own sweet pace, no matter how the interest rates are manipulated. Much more biological production than is now the case should be protected from this market vulnerability, and the most practical way to do so is by having more gardens. A garden economy would provide society with a much safer "social security" than pension money sunk into volatile stock-and-bond markets that can collapse overnight. To understand the seriousness of the situation, newer economics books, such as Herman Daly's and John Cobb's *For the Common Good* (Beacon Press, 1989) and Margrit Kennedy's *Interest and Inflation Free Money* (New Society Publishers, 1995) are helpful—in fact, essential.

Call this new kind of social security an investment in "mutual garden funds." If enough people took up practical food gardening and other kinds of practical craft work in the production of clothing and shelter, more or less free of the enslavement of interest rates, maybe this subeconomy could offset the money madness enough to avert a real catastrophe, ultimately generating a true home economy rather than a money economy. The home economy is based on human interest, not monetary interest.

## How Home Economy Works: Shareholders of Garden "Stocks"

We are taught to invest our savings in stocks and bonds or in mutual funds, which are then invested in stocks and bonds. Perhaps this is a smart thing to do; I surely don't know. The trouble with any of these pieces of paper or metal (other than the fact that *most* people don't have the surplus money to take advantage of them) is that you can't do anything with pieces of paper in times of economic disruption except start fires. It is gambling. If you think for a long time about really safe investments, if there are such things, you may reach the contrary gardener's conclusion: the safest security would come from being part of a caring community of more or less self-sustaining households that share their spare-time labor and their production from this work. We have the technology today to turn a plot of ground as small as a quarter-acre into a tiny garden farm productive enough to provide more than an average family's basic food needs of fruit, vegetables, meat, and eggs. My experience suggests that a community of four-acre homesites could add to this production enough sheep and cows for its own milk, wool, and leather, plus space for craft workshops and aquaculture ponds. A community of ten-acre homesteads could provide more of these resources, plus enough renewable wood for most of the community's heating and furniture needs, and some additional lumber for construction purposes. All that the successful system needs, in addition to the land, is a decent climate and the commitment of its members' spare-time labor.

Community-supported agriculture (CSA) is another way in which food security is being pursued, by combining the garden economy with the outside market economy. Be wary. In many cases, a CSA is just a way—a nicer one to be sure—to get hammered good by the mainstream economy. It is not for everyone. Read Judith Hoffman's exhaustive report on CSAs in the Winter 1996 issue of *Small Farmer's Journal*. Studying her survey, I conclude that it takes a veritable saint to run a CSA successfully. Steve Smith, whose farm in Trimble County, Kentucky, I visited last year, is one of the saints, although he will be embarrassed by my saying so. He devotes three and a half acres of his and his father's tobacco, hay, and livestock farm to vegetables, which he sells to a prepaying "subscription" list of customer-clients. In 1994, the latest year I have his figures for, ninety-two people belonged to his CSA. He charged them $395 each (prepaid) to cover his costs and for risk-sharing the crop. He netted $20,113. Each member got a half-bushel basket of assorted vegetables every week, choosing from whatever was available, usually from ten to fifteen different kinds of vegetables, picking up their allotments at a central location. (Most clients were from Louisville, Kentucky.) "The response from members has been overwhelming," Steve told me. "Our wish and effort to please them sets off this wonderfully dynamic spirit of cooperation rebounding back and forth between us, each trying to outdo the other's kindness, making room for human error and unexpected gifts." Sounds almost too good to be true. He also must have the knack of attracting saintly customers because, believe me, it's not going to be this way all the time.

In 1996 Steve tells me he is adding eggs from his own chickens to his food baskets, which is a perfectly logical thing to do. He says that when skill and good weather come together, a person should figure, as a rule of thumb, that one acre of vegetables sold retail equals $10,000 gross.

I have nothing but admiration for Steve Smith, but I think that for most of us, a much smaller, nonbusiness kind of CSA would work out better. An Amish housewife I know, who modestly asks me not to use her name, operates a mini-CSA out of her garden. She sells to four upscale families whom she came to know personally before inviting them into her garden. They are enchanted with the privilege of being able to bring their children to the farm once a week and not only help pick the produce, but join in the whole life of the farm. "They pay me more than I ask," she says. "It's kind of embarrassing. They are very serious about avoiding chemicals on food, but mainly they just enjoy coming here."

This sort of program might be a delightful alternative for a lot of gardeners. After all, families will often pay $20 or more per member to go to a theme park just once (not counting the food they eat there), and come away with nothing but short tempers. Being allowed to roam your garden paradise, pet and feed your animals, watch the fish in your aquaculture pool (maybe even go swimming), observe your birds and butterflies, pick apples and hickory nuts in your tree grove, press some of their own cider—all this, on a very small scale, might well be worth accepting more renumeration for than what your vegetables are worth in dollars and cents.

## Home Economy: Shareholders of Mutual Equipment Funds

Another way to save money is to share equipment. Even the equipment dealers benefit, although they may not at first see it that way. Instead of each buying one cheap lawnmower or garden tiller, two or more families might go in together and buy one good one. Dividing the cost, they pay less per family than they would to own a cheap model individually. The bigger, more rugged machine will mean that each family can finish mowing or tilling quicker, with fewer breakdowns. The machine will last longer, saving more money, and won't clutter up the landfills so soon. The dealer will make just about as much money selling one $3,000 machine, for example, as two $1,700 ones. Repairing good machines that are rugged enough to make the repair work worthwhile will be just as profitable for the dealer, I daresay, as hiring yet another worker to repair twice as many cheap machines that aren't really worth repairing and which produce a huge headache because of complaining customers.

We share a cider press with four of my sisters and their families, and it works out very well. The apple-pressing season is very long, so each of us can use the press for one weekend at least, with plenty of time for everyone.

Certainly, sharing a good, heavy-duty snowblower can make more sense for three or more nearby homeowners than each neighbor having a dinky little model that takes half the morning to clear one driveway. This is especially true if one of the shareowners has a heated garage in which to keep the blower, so the dang thing starts readily on cold, blizzardy mornings.

Two or three neighbors, each with five acres, say, could share-buy a farm tractor with accessories and, with studied cooperation, do just fine. Like the farmers of my father's era, who shared ownership in all kinds of machinery, they could take turns using the tractor, following a schedule fair to everyone.

Among neighbors who like one another, trading labor often works out well too, since work (especially tedious work, such as putting on a new roof or building a fence) is almost fun when done with a helper or two.

Sometimes trading tools or equipment also is practical. A neighbor borrows your pickup. You borrow her deluxe canner. Nobody keeps a list of who's borrowing the most. This economy requires a little bit of sainthood, too.

## Home Economy: The Seedsaver

Specific to gardening, home economy suggests that contrary gardeners take a long, hard look at the seeds and plants they buy. Not so many years ago, you could buy a 45¢ seed packet with enough seeds in it to supply the whole town with tomatoes. Lately, my seed bill has risen to nearly $60 for just the basic annual vegetables. Like other gardeners on moderate or fixed incomes, I've had to search for better prices as assiduously as I search for better seeds.

For those vegetables and flowers which go to seed annually in your garden, consider becoming a seedsaver. This means that you will switch the focus of your production to heirloom and other open-pollinated varieties, rather than hybrids. Unlike hybrids, seed from open-pollinated varieties reproduces fairly true to its parentage.

The first reason to become a seedsaver is that it immediately saves money, but this is only part of the picture. You will still want to keep on buying open-pollinated varieties and strains from commercial seed companies, simply because they have a larger selection of plants on test, are better trained to select seed from the more promising plants within a variety, and have access to hundreds of varieties not available to you locally. By saving some seed and trading with other growers, the seed business opens up to the kind of communal effort it used to be. Money is saved all around, but by the same token, the chances to make money are increased because there are unlimited possible new strains of low-cost seed when working with open-pollinated varieties. A good example is 'Big Dipper' pepper, offered in 1996 exclusively by Burpee. 'Big Dipper' is an improved open-pollinated strain of open-pollinated 'CaliforniaWonder'. I suppose it was spotted by an observant seed steward and saved; the improvement was done by nature. Since, in my experience 'California Wonder' is an excellent variety, as good as hybrids I've tried, I was eager to test 'Big Dipper' to see if it really was an improvement under my growing conditions. It was. This is better progress than hybridization, in my opinion. Burpee makes money, the original grower who spotted the new strain makes money, and I have seed that I can save. (As a matter of fact, as I'm sure seed houses anticipate, I forgot to save the seed and will have to buy some again.)

In saving seed (or plants, in the case of berries and maybe asparagus), individually nice specimens of fruit or vegetable should not be your only criterion. For example, experiments done nearly a century ago determined that rather than save only large potatoes for seed, one should select seed from the hill(s) that produce the most tubers of good, uniform size. In corn, you would not want to save an ear from a weak, drooping stalk, no matter how nice the ear, but from a strong stalk. And in making the selection, my experience is that you should include seed from several of the nicer plants, not from just one.

Can you save seed from hybrids? It's not supposed to be practical, but it can be interesting to do so. I tried it with popcorn last year and got only one nice ear. The others looked curled and wrinkly, as if they had been listening to pop radio all summer. However, the kernels popped just as well and tasted just as good as on normal ears.

There's another reason to concentrate on open-pollinated seeds. With hybrids, you will eventually be playing into the hands of the food monopolists. Agribusiness megacompanies (such as ConAgra, Cargill, Philip Morris, and so on) have the professed goal of vertically integrating the food business "from seed to shelf." The old homey seed company that you think is owned by that old homey family, with long beards and honest faces on the inside cover of the catalog, likely belongs now to a bunch of wet-behind-the-ears, silk-tie, corporate-business-school whizzes who think marshmallows grow on bushes. The big food companies hope to monopolize the seed business as they have done the commercial seed-corn business, through hybridization, and more frighteningly, through patenting genetically engineered plants. Unfortunately this is the real world that commercial growers may have to face.

But not contrary gardeners.

Lest you think I sound paranoid, here is what two respected evolutionary biologists, Richard Lewontin and Jean-Pierre Berian, write in a book called *Agroecology* (McGraw-Hill, 1990): "The development of hybrid corn is a paradigm case of the way in which the channeling of research in one direction rather than another has been the consequence of the power of one group to capture the social returns of that research by the production of a commodity of very high value. A rational alternative to the inbred-hybrid method existed (mass selection) and was deliberately and self-consciously put aside in order to create superprofits for seed producers."

If you want to save seed, you must be careful not to plant certain vegetables close to one another. The plants this year might look and taste okay, but weird things can happen when you plant their seed if they have inadvertently cross-pollinated with the wrong vegetable. One year, before I knew better, I planted 'Delicata' squash next to yellow squash and acorn squash. The following year, the 'Delicata' seed that I had saved fruited the most grotesque creatures that ever appeared in our garden. They had crossed with the yellow squash and maybe the acorn squash, and though the results made great conversation-stoppers for fall decoration, they had the consistency, even when cooked, of a chunk of white pine. You can get similar problems with two kinds of cucumbers or two kinds of melons planted next to each other, although crosses between two cucumbers or two melons could lead to something better. Sweet corn of any kind will cross with field corn, popcorn, or Indian corn close to it, and produce odd stuff the next year, perhaps accompanied by loss of taste in the sweet corn and less pop to the popcorn. However, you can usually get away with planting early- and late-season varieties of corn next to each other because their pollination times will not coincide. Of course, sometimes you might get a sensational new creation instead. Perhaps a chicken passing one of your more amorous cucumber vines will begin to lay pickles instead of eggs.

Biennials produce seed only in their second year, and in regions they don't winter over they are difficult to get seed from. Carrots, beets, and onions can be dug up, stored over winter, and set out again the next spring to go to seed. But that's hardly worth the effort. Parsley and kale can be mulched over mild winters; they will usually grow a second year and flower.

Dry seeds (such as those of beans, peas, and corn) are harvested after the pods or ears are themselves completely dry. Store them in a cool, dry place, or in a deep freeze if seed maggots or weevils are a problem. Seeds of melons, squash, cucumbers, tomatoes, and eggplant (but not peppers), as well as fruit seeds, are harvested wet from the fruity flesh around them. For best results, these seeds should be allowed to soak awhile in their own fermenting juices, to which you can add a little water. The good seeds will sink to the bottom and the bad ones will float. After two to four days of fermentation, pour off the water with any floating seeds, then strain the good seeds and dry them for storage. They will clump together when dry, but can be easily and gently rubbed apart. Tree-fruit seeds can be planted right into a mulch bed after the fermenting process, rather than stored, and they will sprout and grow the following spring, if not sooner.

Though hardly anyone does it, you can plant seed from almost any tree, including fruit trees, and get nice specimens for free. Thousands of oak and maple trees come up from seed in our lawn and grove every spring. The hitch, in the case of fruit trees at least, is that the seeds won't necessarily produce a tree exactly like the parent. It might not be as good, but then again, it could be better. The trees planted from seed will all have standard, natural rootstock of course, which means that they will grow into natural-sized trees. But this is also to my liking, as I now avoid most dwarf trees because of their weak root systems.

## Still More Home Economy: The Careful Shopper

I frankly can't understand the continuous outpouring of how-to garden books. The garden industry has improved its catalogs so marvelously that right within their pages, you can learn all the basic stuff about how to grow a garden. Of course, you have also to wade through hyperbolic, meaningless descriptions of the plants offered for sale. After awhile, the purple prose gets as thick as possum-fat gravy, and salting it down with all those worn-out superlatives doesn't make it taste any better. I would hate to be the unfortunate people who have to write those blurbs. Seed companies should preface their catalogs with this announcement:

> All the varieties offered herein are the best, most productive, most weather-tolerant, most tasty, and most attractive that we have to offer, or we wouldn't offer them. Otherwise, they are varieties that our stubborn customers demand, even if the results are not all that great. The photos we use to depict fruits and vegetables are merely pretty pictures, and do not necessarily look like the variety being offered. Or they represent that variety only in the way you represent yourself when dressed up for a presidential ball. We could save you and us lots of money by dispensing with these stupid pictures, but experience has taught us that our customers insist on the right to be lied to.

Such as disclaimer would take care of the hyperbole, so that the catalogs could be used for truly pertinent or amusing or intriguing details about gardening. Some catalogs are becoming more informative, with nice pencil drawings of the various species of fruits and vegetables. I salute particularly those catalogs that make room for personal recipes or ways to fix garden food. Shepherd's Garden Seeds, for example, throws in unusual recipes between its seed offerings. The recipe for "Celebration Fresh Tomato Bisque" is prefaced by this note: "First made for the engagement dinner of our talented graphic artist Linda Lane by her wonderful fiance, Will." Who could resist a catalog with a heart like that? Also in Shepherd's, I found (for the first time) proof that catalogs can be honest: a little item about how to store unused seeds in cool, dry quarters so they will be viable the next year. It takes real character to educate the customer when it would benefit the company's grosser instincts to hope the seeds didn't remain viable, in order to sell more.

It is surprising how many garden accessories, tools, and strange inventions you can find in addition to seeds and plants, if you search assiduously through enough catalogs. Since you are going to be inundated with the catalogs anyway, you might as well get some good out of them before burning them in your woodstove. Read them all closely. If you get Gurney's, or Jung's, or similar newspaper-sized catalogs, you will be obliged to read them closely because the various offerings are crammed together like maggots in a dead chicken. Only by looking closely can you separate the chaff from the grain. And that's part of the fun, too. You soon learn that small pictures do not mean insignificant offerings. Gurney's, for example, was only one of two catalogs (out of the several zillions that littered our mailbox this spring) that carried soil-block makers, which I was particularly interested in. The other was Gardener's Supply. I expect to see the latest in Gardener's Supply, because it always seems to have its eye peeled on the horizon, but I was surprised to find Gurney's just as aware of the new. I had classed Gurney's as a more conservative outfit, still selling wonderful old things like 'Mammoth Red Mangels' that no one under the age of ninety-seven has ever seen.

Wildly imaginative plant aids and accessories can pop up anywhere in today's garden catalog world. In Jung's I find the "Automator," which looks like a little plastic tray, but for which almost magical power is claimed. An Automator fits around a young plant and "its collar protects against cutworms; blossom end rot is reduced; its black color absorbs heat and warms the soil, serves as a mulch to prevent weed growth and retain moisture." Meanwhile, water poured into it "feeds slowly and evenly" into the ground underneath. For a gardener, items like this make leafing through catalogs akin to browsing through *Sports Illustrated*'s swimsuit edition. It's not that we are going to buy them—just look at them.

Another recent trend I like is the catalog that concentrates on a particular plant species, and endeavors to offer a very extensive selection of that species. For example, Seeds for the World, now combined with the Vermont Bean Seed Company, offers ninety-six (if I counted right) different varieties of beans. Think of that: ninety-six different ways to generate biogas. The company also offers a "Totally Tomatoes" catalog, offering over three hundred varieties of the love apple plus one hundred varieties of peppers.

I'd better say somewhere that no garden catalog is paying me to mention it, or even wants me to. As a former mayor of our town said to me when I offered to support his re-election bid in my local and sometimes controversial newspaper column, "Thanks, Gene, but please don't."

The problem with all the goodies in the garden catalogs is that you can easily overinvest to the point where your garden costs you more than the food you get from it. Of course, this is also true when you dine at an expensive French restaurant where you have to wear your reading glasses to find the food on your plate.

On the other hand, you really can save money if you study your catalogs closely. For example, some seed companies have realized that most gardeners only want a few plants of each variety, so they are selling packets with only a few seeds in them, at prices that are 30 to 50 percent cheaper than the conventional packet. Pinetree Garden Seeds is an example. A packet of 'California Wonder' pepper seeds with a minimum of twenty seeds per packet costs 40¢ from Pinetree. From Gurney, you can buy a packet of 'California Wonder' with one hundred seeds to the packet, for $1.15. Per seed, Gurney is cheaper. But if you only want ten to twenty pepper plants, Pinetree is a more efficient purchase.

Buying garden seeds is not as straightforward a shopping exercise as you might think. The catalogers play games with us, knowing that we enjoy whiling away the winter evenings trying to outwit them. You need to have a lot of floor space to go catalog seed-shopping. Spread out around you a half-dozen of your favorite catalogs—more, if you want to play the game to the hilt. Get out a pencil and pad, and seat yourself in the middle of the catalogs. You are now ready to figure cost comparisons in detail. Let us, for the sake of example, shop for 'Sweet 100' cherry tomato seed, since nearly everyone seems to carry it (very good variety, by the way). Now go from catalog to catalog, being careful not just to compare prices, but quantities in relation to prices. For reasons only the seed houses know, the number of seeds per packet is not uniform across the trade, nor do all merchandisers sell in units of the same weight. Some companies sell by the packet only (with invitations to ask about whole-sale prices for large lots). Hybrid seed packets usually contain consider-ably less seed than packets of open-pollinated seed do. Some companies offer, in addition to packets, half-pound and one-pound packages, and sometimes five-pound packages. Other vendors offer quantities in ounces or fractions of ounces. When you compare, you need to be sure you are comparing like amounts. It can get tricky.

So, with your pencil and pad, proceed to list the companies and their price quotations. For one packet of hybrid 'Sweet 100' in the spring of 1996, here was my comparison:

| Company | Single-Packet | Quantity and Price | Additional Quantities |
|---|---|---|---|
| Burpee | 30 seeds | $1.75 | 2 packets for $2.95 |
| Gurney | 30 seeds | $1.62 | more packets for $1.47 each |
| Seeds for the World | 30 seeds | $1.45 | |
| The Cook's Garden | 25 seeds | $1.90 | |
| Shepherd's | 30 to 40 seeds* | $1.95 | |
| Pinetree | 12 seeds minimum† | $0.95 | |
| Jung | number not given‡ | $1.45 | 2 packets for $2.50; 5 packets for $5.45; 10 packets for $8.90 |

In some tomato varieties, Jung (and others) offer tiny seeds in frac-tions of ounces, or they may throw you a curve and use grams. Thanks to the Cook's Garden catalog, I know that one ounce of tomato seed

---

* Shepherd's calls their seed 'Sweet 100 Plus,' which may be improved 'Sweet 100.'

† Pinetree offers 'Sweet Million' here, not 'Sweet 100,' but the two varieties are similar, and both did well in my garden.

‡ Probably 30, the usual number given for their other packets of hybrid tomato seed, but not always.

equals approximately 8,000 seeds. One gram equals approximately 250 seeds. So there are about 250 seeds in 1/32 of an ounce, a common unit offered for sale.

The exact or nearly exact number of seeds per package may not be particularly important to you if you sow your rows in the garden in the conventional manner. But if you are starting plants in containers or soil blocks, seed count can become very important in saving money.

It is interesting to run a comparison using peas. Consider 'Green Arrow' peas:

| Company | Single-Packet | Quantity and Price | Additional Quantities |
|---|---|---|---|
| Burpee | 200 to 225 seeds | $1.45 | ½ lb. $3.25 |
| | | | 1 lb. $4.95 |
| | | | 2 lb. $8.45 |
| | | | 5 lb. $16.95 |
| The Cook's Garden | 250 seeds (2 oz.) | $2.10 | ½ lb. $5.25 |
| | | | 1 lb. $8.40 |
| Seeds for the World | ¼ lb. | $1.85 | ½ lb. $2.95 |
| | | | 1 lb. $4.75 |
| | | | 2 lbs. $8.50 |
| | | | 5 lbs. $14.75 |
| Pinetree | 250 seeds (2 oz.) | $0.85 | 8 packets (1 lb.) $6.80 |
| Jung | "generous" 2 oz. | $0.95 | ½ lb. $2.55 |
| | | | 1 lb. $4.25 |
| | | | 2 lbs. $6.95 |
| | | | 4 lbs. $11.95 |
| Gurney | 2 oz. | $1.15 | 2 or more packets |
| | | | $1.04 each; ½ lb. $2.79; |
| | | | 2 or more $2.50 each; |
| | | | 2 lbs. $8.20; |
| | | | 2 or more $7.45 each |

Obviously prices do vary, sometimes significantly so. In addition to just comparing prices, your job is to study your lists bearing in mind the quantity of seed that you need. Can you get by with two packets of peas rather than a half-pound? If so, you save a little even though the half-pound package provides a cheaper per pea price. And so on.

Some catalogs complicate things further (to your advantage) by offering specials of two or more units of different varieties together at a reduced price. Thus Gurney offers a packet of 'Green Arrow' and a packet of 'Little Marvel' together at a savings of 45¢ over the listed price of each. Or you can buy "Grandma Gurney's Herb Garden" (don't you just love that?) of five packets of different herbs, for a savings of $1.06 over the listed prices of each. I bit on a special offering of a packet of 'Kandy Korn' (my favorite sugar-enhanced corn) and one of 'Bodacious', a new variety that I was curious about. The savings was 69¢, and since I bought a double special, I saved $1.38. Where specials like this really save is in ordering larger quantities. Two pounds of each variety on this special would save $5.59 over the listed price.

But (there is always a "but," and my editor scolds me for using too many of them) you have to figure in any handling costs and possible sales taxes when you make price comparisons. Not only does the price of handling vary from company to company, but it adds up to a considerable expense if you are only buying a couple of packets of seed from each one.

The sales-tax law regarding mail-order seeds is really stupid. If the seed company is headquartered in your state or a state contiguous to yours, you have to pay the applicable sales tax, which can add considerably to a big order. So what happens is that all of us contrary gardeners order most of our seeds from companies in states not contiguous to ours. The law is twice dumb because many seeds that you receive from a seed company's headquarters did not even originate there. I can facetiously visualize a situation in which a seed broker buys seed from a grower, who pays taxes on it, and then sells the same seed to a mail-order company, who pays taxes on it again. Then the same seed is purchased by a gardener, who again pays taxes on it. By now the tax has amounted to about as much as the seed is worth. No wonder seed prices keep climbing! Enterprising mail-order seed companies will probably start headquartering in Alaska, which has no states contiguous to it.

# CHAPTER 4

# THE HARDLY-EVER-TILLED GARDEN: THE MULCH BED

Nature has practiced mulch-bed gardening in the forest and on the prairie forever. Every year the old leaves and grasses fall and rot into humus. The soil becomes the living bread-broth of all life. No cultivation takes place; no dirt is stirred annually. Seeds drop and plant themselves (squirrels and birds help). Given a climate favorable to plant growth, the earth would continue to increase in fertility indefinitely by this process, were it not for the unnatural interference of human short-sightedness. The ecosystem of forest or prairie is disturbed by natural fire and lava occasionally, but the burned area, reduced to ash, gets a new start, blooms with a great diversity of species, and returns slowly to its climax trees or grass.

In mulch-bed gardening, we mimic this process. Every year, we cover the soil surface with more organic matter—leaves usually, but anything that will rot into humus and provide nutrients. Seeds or plants are placed into this duff of rotting organic matter, and the soil surface is not otherwise disturbed. No double-digging or even single-digging is necessary, nor do the beds need to be artificially raised. Once every five to ten years, the mulch bed is mechanically cultivated for a year, taking the place of fire in nature, to break up disease, pest, and weed cycles. Or, in the case of asparagus or grain stubble after harvest, the bed can be literally burned over, mimicking the forest fire.

Wise gardeners have practiced this mimicry of nature for centuries, I suppose. The first explicit description of it that I have found in modern times is in a 1915 book, *Home Gardening* (Grosset & Dunlap), by Benjamin Albaugh, referred to in some detail later in this chapter. Ruth

Stout popularized the practice in the 1960s in *Organic Gardening* magazine, and Stu Campbell (see his article "Magnificent Mulch" in *Kitchen Garden* magazine April/May, 1996) has continued to do so. Bill Mollison's *Permaculture* books (Tagari Community Books, 1978, 1979), and scores of other books, have encouraged the idea. Still, mulch-bed gardening, which is kind of a lazy man's version of French intensive gardening (no digging), is not as common as conventionally cultivated gardens. I think this is partly the case because not enough mulch has been easily available until recently, when towns could no longer burn leaves and so started making them available to gardeners from yard-waste composting operations. Another reason why mulch-bed gardening has not been more popular may be that it is too simple: The typical gardener does not think he or she is working except when throwing dirt around with piston-ringed roarers.

I started laying out mulch beds when I noticed that compacted soil was forming at about six inches below the soil surface in the garden, just below the depth of the tiller tines. It's an old story. The action of the plow in clayish soils, exacerbated by heavy farm equipment, also forms that hard layer at plow depth. Farmers call it plowpan or hardpan. Disks will cause it too—even chisel plows. Deep-rooting crops in rotation keep hardpan from becoming a problem, but in my garden, I had thought I could dispense with such rotations. Who would have thought that a garden tiller could do this? I was reminded once more that mechanics and biology are inherently in conflict. Those old superstitions about the steel plow poisoning the soil weren't all that wrong.

So, with the intention of planting my compacted garden plot to alfalfa for a year (or letting dandelions take over because of their deep taprooting ability), I needed to dig up a new plot in the lawn while the present plot was being revitalized. The prospect of bouncing the tiller around on that thick sod was about as enticing as working up a seedbed on an old mattress. Spading was even less enticing. What the heck—I'd just cover the sod with six inches of leaf mulch, and then dig small holes down through the mulch with the shovel or posthole digger to set tomato transplants in. I'd done that years ago, and it had worked okay.

To make a long story short, this untilled mulch-bed gardening

47

worked marvelously well. In the hottest summer on record here, while vegetables in other parts of the garden were withering, those tomatoes in the mulch bed strutted right along to an adequate harvest. All I did was add a second layer of leaves when some weeds and grass tried to poke up through the first layer, and then plop forkfuls of manure bedding from the barn on the few weeds that tried again to reach daylight.

I asked myself, Why not grow the whole garden this way?

There was another reason for trying to do so. Commercial farm soils are heavily treated with chemical nitrogen, phosphorus, and potash, and the lush plants induced by this fertilizer tend to draw out of the soil its native supply of micronutrients. Alarming reports have been coming forth in the last two decades, contending that food from this kind of agriculture is becoming deficient in trace minerals such as zinc, copper, iron, manganese, selenium, cobalt, and chromium—all essential in minute quantities for good health. Heavy applications of manure or compost are the best way to recharge soils deficient in these micronutrients, or to keep soils from getting deficient in the first place.

One more reason drew me to mulch-bed gardening. I had been reading statistics (probably a dangerous thing to do, since all manipulations of numbers beyond pure mathematics turn out to be half-truths at best), and it seems that per square foot, homeowners use more herbicides and motor fuel on lawns and gardens than farmers do on grain crops and pastures. Even if this analysis is not completely true (depends on which group of homeowners you survey), what an indictment. Farmers at least can say that they have to use chemicals and petroleum products because they must compete in an industrial economy. Home residents can only justify such extravagance as pandering to their sense of neatness. In their minds, nature must not escape the Prussian dictum of order and duty. Nature must be manhandled by chemicals and machines and, heaven help us, kept arrow-straight with yardstick and row strings, until the gardener has a heart attack or quits gardening because "it's too strenuous," as I often hear. It would not surprise me if the famous philosopher, Immanuel Kant, with his stern philosophy of hewing to duty above all, invented double-digging.

Besides, I was growing tired of loud, demanding piston engines. They were trying to rule my life with noise and constant need for maintenance. I realized with dismay that there were eight fossil-fueled motors on our farm: two tractors plus the ancient walk-behind Gravely mower-tiller, a car, a pickup truck, two lawnmowers, and a garden tiller. At least one of these machines was always in need of repair. Thinking about the expense and the time and the mental distress that they exacted from me, I concluded that contrary gardening should concern itself not just with the laziest way to grow food, but in addition, with a way that depended more on peaceful and possibly less laborious hand work than being dragged around by piston-ringed roarers.

Of course, hauling leaves and other mulching materials requires some use of piston power too, from the pickup truck. But I need the truck for other transportation purposes anyway, and at least that rusting, 6-cylinder workhorse has gone along now for sixteen years without causing me any mechanical tribulations. Also, by using lots of yard wastes on our garden, we help our village avoid some of the horrendous cost (taxes) of hauling and composting or landfilling the stuff.

But what really convinced me that mulch-bed gardening was here to stay on my place occurred in 1996, the Year From Hell, as it is referred to in northern Ohio. March was cold and rainy. April was cold and rainy. May was cold and rainy. June was (are you ready for this?) cold and rainy. Sometime in May, I lost what little patience I normally have. Okay, so nature wanted to play cold and rainy; I'd garden cold and rainy. I dropped seed potatoes in the mud (no, I'm not exaggerating) and covered them with six inches of straw. I wallowed around in one of the previous year's mulch beds until I had smeared the new strawberry plants into place. On the surface of another mulch bed, I dribbled pea seeds and stepped them into good contact with the mulch duff (as if that latter exercise were necessary in the steady rain). Behold, they quickly sprouted, and I then covered the sprouts with three inches of loose, unrotted leaves to discourage weeds. No cultivation whatsoever. Eventually, I even planted some corn, beans, beets, and carrots this way. The onion sets I just jammed in the mud, cursing the foul clouds. When rain continued,

I also damned tomato, pepper, cabbage, and eggplant into a mire of mud and weeds (of course the weeds were growing merrily), and then between showers, mulched around them heavily, smothering the weeds.

That mess of mire and mulch turned out to grow one of our best gardens ever, even though, and this is the real bottom line—in July the rains stopped abruptly, and the weather turned hot and dry for the rest of the summer. The soil surface of commercial farm fields around us baked as hard as a superhighway, but our mulch beds remained big sponges. The potatoes grew right up through the straw mulch, and when weeds tried to follow, I spread a layer of leaf mulch over them and the straw. The peas came up more or less weedless through their layer of loose leaves. In July, when the crop was about finished, I set out kale plants among the old vines and mulched around them, covering the pea growth, which thereby became fertile green manure. Again, no cultivation. We were still eating the kale at Christmas time.

The asparagus, growing in a permanent mulch bed, did fine in the cold, wet weather. So did the rhubarb. Bibb lettuce, planted in a little mulch bed around which I had erected a cold frame, did best of all, protected early from the cold by the cold frame's glass. The strawberries survived mud-mulch transplanting fairly well. The raspberries, prospering on a well-drained mulch bed, did not get the go-backs as they often will in wet years. Cabbage, peppers, and broccoli were slow to start, but when the hot weather came, they burst with vitality (literally, in the case of the cabbage). Only some experimental corn and pole beans planted together early in a mulch bed did not do well, and this was because I mulched too quickly, before the soil was warm enough for corn.

So I was hooked on mulch beds. Their other great advantage, as I soon learned, was that formal rows were unnecessary. I could set plants much more densely, which meant that my plantings also shaded out weeds more effectively. Also, succession planting became much easier, since I could start new plants before the current crop was finished. For these reasons, I could reduce the overall area of the garden. *The smaller the garden area, the more practical mulch bed gardening becomes.*

This ability to reduce the size of the garden while maintaining or actually increasing production is most important because mulching is primarily handwork, and so it is physically easy to do only in small plots. Benjamin Albaugh, who maintained this kind of mulch-bed garden in the early 1900s, (he called it the "gardenette"), claimed in his book cited earlier that in a space of four square rods (about eleven hundred square feet), he grew this astounding yield: 30 dozen green onions; 1 bushel of dry onions; 10 messes of peas (I guess a "mess" is a meal's worth); 15 dozen beets, 22 dozen radishes; 200 heads of celery; 25 eggplants; 25 squashes; 50 messes of lettuce; 20 messes of endive; 10 messes of kohlrabi; 8 dozen ears of sweet corn; 10 messes of green beans; 25 heads of cauliflower; 25 heads of cabbage; 20 messes of spinach; 10 messes of chard; 20 messes of asparagus; 10 messes of salsify; 10 dozen carrots; 10 dozen parsnips; 50 muskmelons; 200 pickling cucumbers; 10 slicing cucumbers; 5 bushels of tomatoes; 2 bushels of early potatoes; 8 quarts of lima beans; 3 bushels of turnips; 3 quarts of okra; and 3 dozen sweet peppers.

## Mulching Basics

### What to Use as Mulch

Last year's leaves make the best mulch because they are available in quantity, cheap or free for the hauling. They are not yet mature compost, and therefore work better for weed control. They break down relatively fast and are fairly free of weed seed. Alternate them occasionally with bedding manure, if you can get it, or finished compost. Our village gives away last fall's leaves and will even load your pickup with its front-end loader. These leaves have already begun to compost and may smell a little (not bad, more like curing tobacco), but after you get them spread out on the garden, the odor goes away.

Commercial composts, made from yard wastes, are good but perhaps too expensive to use in the quantities necessary for mulch-bed gardening. Grass clippings are cheaper, and excellent if not raked from a lawn that has been treated with weedkillers recently. The grass mulch won't mat too much, and therefore won't keep rain from penetrating into the ground.

Light rains may be absorbed by the mulch and not do the soil underneath much good, but light rains do very little in the way of watering plants anyhow.

The more significant sources of water for summer gardens are the winter and spring rains that saturate the soil. Then capillary action during summer draws the soil moisture from below, and mulch saves more of this moisture for plant use than it absorbs from light rains. Heavy summer rains will penetrate the matted mulch. More importantly, the rainwater will flow down through the mulch where the plants come up through it—right where you want the water to go. And in dry climates where irrigation is necessary, mulch placed over drip-water lines reduces evaporation, and therefore reduces at least by half the amount of water needed.

Straw makes good mulch, and doesn't mat, but you usually have to contend with sprouting wheat in the straw. Old hay, too low in quality for animal feed, works okay, but may have weed seeds in it. Salt hay is excellent. Good clover or alfalfa hay contains significant amounts of minerals and plant food, but good hay is better used as animal feed, and the resulting manure used for mulch.

Keep in mind that fresh manure soaked with urine will burn plants it comes into contact with. When I use fresh manure, I lay it a few inches away from the plants, and when it dries after a day or two, I tuck it up around the plants. Well-shredded corn stalks are excellent for mulching, and rice hulls work out especially well for applying around and up next to closely spaced plants, such as strawberries.

Algae and seaweed make unexpectedly worthwhile mulches. I had figured that gathering the algae from our pond and using it for mulch would be too laborious to be practical, but this prediction has not proven correct. My pleasant summer Sunday job is skimming the excess algae from the pond with a pitch fork and tossing it up on the pond bank. In a few days, the algae dries to a light, clothlike material, easy to gather up and spread around plants.

Shredded bark is useful mulch, if allowed to compost for a year or two. Sawdust also needs to rot down before use. However, commercial mulches typically applied around ornamental plantings are not good for the produce garden: They are composed mostly of fairly large flakes of ground-up wood, and do not break down into humus fast enough to nourish food plants.

The first time you turn a garden plot into a mulch bed, you should consider mulching with bedding manure if you can get it, or finished compost, so as to get a good, rich duff of nitrogenous organic matter on the soil surface before piling on unrotted or half-rotted leaves. Starting with leaf mulch only, the leaves might rob the plants of nitrogen during the first year, although they usually don't do this in any kind of healthy soil. After the first year and the longer a bed is annually mulched, the richer it gets, and you do not need to worry about temporary nitrogen depletion from unrotted leaves.

Whether or not you raise your beds, the benefits of simple mulch-bed gardening are numerous, as noted throughout this chapter. New benefits constantly reveal themselves, too. For example, mulch-bed gardening prevents mud from splattering up on edible parts of fruits and vegetables. This advantage alone is worth the effort, in my opinion.

### When and How to Mulch

The most important rule of mulching is not to add a layer of new mulch (four to six inches is my standard) until the soil has warmed up and plants are growing well—in other words not until vegetables (or weeds) have sprouted and grow vigorously. Mulching any earlier in spring than this, or late in the preceding fall, will keep clay soils from drying and warming up until June (where I live). Can't have that.

Also, don't use more mulch to control weeds than you need. In the first place, you want to stretch your supply of mulching material as far as possible. Second, it is good to go into winter, or at least come out of winter, with most of the mulch rotted down to humus, so that the soil underneath freezes a little to kill pest bugs, and then warms up fast in spring before planting. Too thick a mulch layer won't properly decompose.

The old mulch layer from the preceding year should have (in a moderately humid climate as prevails in most of the eastern two-thirds of the

U.S.) rotted down to only an inch or two of crumbly organic duff by spring. This duff, being dark in color, absorbs the warmth of the spring sun and so is ready for planting a little earlier than normal. It can actually take the place of black plastic used for that purpose. If weeds also come early, don't worry about them. If they get too tall before you want to set plants in a particular bed, mow them off with the lawnmower. Then set the transplants. When your plants have taken hold well, indicating that the soil is now warm enough, add your current year's mulch around them, blotting out the weeds.

Direct-seeding of early crops (such as radishes, beets, peas, and early beans) should be done as described earlier, right on the soil surface. Step them down or pat them down with a hoe; let them sprout; and then spread a *thin* covering of unrotted shredded leaves over the row. All these direct-seeded crops, except carrots, can be started as transplants and set into the mulch bed later (see chapter 5). The crop seedlings will come up through the leaves, but weeds will be slowed until the crop plants are tall enough to allow you to mulch around them heavily. For later direct-seeded plantings, as of corn or carrots, you *may* want to run the tiller *lightly* over the old mulch to set back weeds. After the corn and carrots are up, then you can mulch around them. A little hand-weeding will often be necessary, especially around carrots, but this is true of conventionally tilled gardens, too.

### Maintaining the Mulch Bed

Nothing lasts forever in life, nor in gardening. A "permanent" mulch bed should be worked up about once every seven years and planted to a crop such as sweet corn where you can do conventional weed cultivation with the tiller ,or hoe between the rows for a year. Then follow the corn with a broadcast seeding of a small grain/legume mixture (see chapter 6 on grain gardening). This rotation helps control certain weeds, including purslane and chickweed, that can build up in a mulch bed over time.

Untilled gardening systems lend themselves to very effective weed control with intermittent use of the herbicide Roundup. Instead of periodically rotating the bed to a clean cultivated crop and a legume, the nonorganic grower can spray the bed in spring before setting out garden plants, and kill all emerging weeds effectively. This method works particularly well to get rid of sow thistles and dandelions that emerge early. (Sow thistles and Canada thistles, which spread by root as well as seed, are extremely difficult to control, even with persistent hand-weeding or machine cultivation. Pull a thistle, and three more pop up from the broken roots.) Roundup, used once every seven years, may seem an affront to organic growers, but it is as close to harmless to the ecosystem as a chemical weed poison can be.

To avoid compaction, some gardeners keep their mulch beds narrow enough that they can reach to the middle from either side. But you can't hurt an older mulch bed by walking on it even when it is gurgling wet from a downpour.

Should you go all out and raise your beds? Where you have no way to relieve a wet garden with tile drainage, raised beds have a practical purpose, especially for early crops. But raised beds are a liability in dry weather, for they require watering sooner than conventional gardens. I can't figure out any agronomic rationale for saying that raised beds grow better food, any more than double-digging does. Turning soil *over* is a cultural fixation (like ritual circumcision), not a horticultural necessity. Mulch beds do rise slightly over time from all that decaying organic matter, so eventually I guess you could call them a form of raised-bed gardening. And raised beds have this to justify them: Even at just six inches higher than the surrounding pathways, it is easier to lean over and work in them.

Another plus for mulch beds is that if you plant heirloom, open-pollinated varieties, their seedlings come up the next year in the mulch. A few can be allowed to grow, or can be potted for use elsewhere. I have to laugh at myself about how much work I put into growing early tomato plants under glass, when by June the volunteer tomato plants in the mulch beds are nearly as big as the ones I set out. These volunteers seldom yield quite as well, and take a little longer to mature, but at an age when your strength is waning, you might turn to them in order to cultivate an everlasting garden that you never have to plant *at all*. Lettuce, melons, potatoes, and tomatoes especially lend themselves to everlasting gardening, while dill and other herbs can become veritable pests in this manner.

## Specific Crops

The basic practice of mulch-bed gardening is generally the same for all vegetables, berries, and trees, but some observations about specific crops can be helpful.

### Asparagus Beds

Most gardeners grow asparagus in permanent mulch beds, and so already have had their introduction to the method. A friend just told me his bed is fifty years old and still producing. This is the best evidence I can present for the practicality of untilled mulch gardening.

Mulch-bed asparagus is difficult to keep free of volunteer asparagus seedlings, which for all practical purposes are weeds. If you can get all-male plants to start with, so I keep hearing, you can avoid this problem. Yet I have tried twice to buy "all-male" plants, and evidently the companies that sell them use a different dictionary than I do. My dictionary says that an all-male plant doesn't produce seeds, but the "all-male" asparagus plants that I buy do so. I keep waiting for these plant suppliers to explain this mystery. To add insult to injury, the "all-male" plants do not grow as vigorously here as the conventional old 'Martha Washington' variety.

The best way to control asparagus "weedlings" and other weeds is with a six-inch covering of leaves, after the asparagus plants have started shooting new stalks in the spring. Then, at some point in late May or June, I get down on my hands and knees, and knead the mulch. By kneading, I mean simply grabbing the mulch by fistfuls and sort of stirring it up. Not much muscle power is needed to destroy most tiny fragile weeds and asparagus weedlings. Later in the year a stray redroot or sourdock will need to be pulled out, but that is about all the care necessary.

In early spring, I burn off the old asparagus stalks. Should a dry spell come along before the new stalks start shooting, I may go over the bed with the tiller *lightly*, just scraping the surface, not deep enough to disturb the roots. If I get this job done, I usually don't have to do much kneading. I often put a second layer of mulch—stable manure—on the bed in late summer.

## Corn and Bean Beds

I am so addicted to growing corn in rows, in comparatively large quantities, and using cultivation for weed control, that it has been hard for me to think of the grain as a potted plant set into a mulch bed. But corn can be transplanted into mulch beds when you want to make small, consecutive plantings. In small plantings, you can forget about rows. Hills of four corn plants, started in a half-gallon milk carton, can be spaced eighteen inches apart in all directions, in very rich soil. When you set the carton into the mulch bed, tear out the bottom, of course, so the roots can grow on into the bed. Let the top of the carton stick up about an inch and a half above the soil surface, to keep out cutworms. This may sound like a laborious way to plant corn, but four plants to a carton (or four stalks per hill) should yield six to eight ears. Ten such hills would grow sixty to eighty ears, about all the corn any family would want ripening at the same time.

Growing common vegetables in pots and setting them out allows for new (very old) concepts in gardening. You are not obliged to think in Prussian and Anglo-Saxon rows. Set out a four-stalk hill of corn, and then, on either side of it, set two pots with a pole bean in each. Sort of a bean-and-corn maypole will result, as the bean vines climb up the central corn stalks. In this arrangement, the climbing beans do better than when planted in a regular corn patch, where the beans are apt to be shaded too much by the corn. The other advantage is that you can pretend you have engineered a real maypole, and in the privacy of your garden, you can dance around it in sexual frolic the way the supposedly puritanical early colonists did. (The Puritans thought they had to have all those horrid blue laws—maypole frolics worried them particularly—because at heart they were delightful pagans.)

### Pepper and Eggplant Beds

Peppers and eggplant, handled just like tomatoes, will grow well in mulch beds, but use more mulch as these two vegetables do not produce a dense mass of foliage to help shade out weeds.

### Potato Beds

The easiest crop for mulch beds is potatoes. Just lay the seed potatoes on the ground, and cover them with about six inches of mulch—straw is better here, too. After the plants come up, put on another four-inch layer of bedding manure, if you have it, or any mulch that is denser than straw. This second denser mulch keeps sunlight from penetrating and turning the potatoes green. At harvest, pull back the mulch and pick up the potatoes. Sometimes mice and other varmints get into potatoes raised this way, but sometimes they get into potatoes raised the conventional way, too.

### Raspberry, Blueberry, and Blackberry Beds

Cane fruits—those wonderful berries—are relatively easy to grow in mulch beds, because the mulch can be tossed in among the canes without fear of covering them after they grow up a foot or so. Because these plants can't tolerate dry weather at fruiting time, mulch is especially beneficial as a substitute for irrigation. My experience is that a cane-fruit bed can be kept vigorous for about four years, and then a new bed should be set out. Dig one-year-old canes from around the edges of the old bed, and transplant them into an entirely new bed. The second-year canes from these transplants will have nice, plump berries. Each year, the canes will get longer, requiring more pruning and more trellising, while the berries will increase in number but decrease in size.

Like strawberries, cane fruits want to move out into new ground every year, and will do so if allowed. Therefore, you can let the old bed start a new bed without actual transplanting. In about the third year of a bed, you will notice a sufficient quantity of new plants growing up in the spring, a couple of feet outside the established bed. Mulch around these new plants as they grow, and rotary-till the old canes in the old bed after the early summer harvest. The old bed can then be used to set out late vegetables or flowers.

Blueberries respond extremely well to rather thick leaf-mulching. If you have acidic mulch, such as pine needles or oak leaves, use them around your blueberries.

## Rhubarb Beds

We have four rhubarb plants, and one would be enough. I put six inches of manure around them every spring. That's all there is to rhubarb care; it's the easiest plant to grow. Its huge leaves lap out and shade away late-growing weeds. Every ten years or so, you should probably dig your rhubarb up and replant just one piece of the rootbound mess you'll find. But we never have. Nor did my mother. We're talking about something close to eighty years of almost no-care rhubarb between us.

## Strawberry Beds

Strawberries are a natural for mulch-bed gardening. That's the way most people grow them, in fact, whether they call it mulch-bed gardening or something else. Plants can be set into the mulch bed almost any time. You are not pushed by the weather to prepared a cultivated bed in early spring, when the soil is still too wet, as often happens at conventional strawberry-planting time. In fact, you don't have to set out plants at all, although this is the best way to get a bumper crop the next year. Runners from an old patch can be allowed to grow out from this year's producing plants, root of their own accord, and become the main bearing plants for next year. Weak old plants should be removed, or covered with mulch and thereby destroyed. If you set the new plants off to the side in a sort of row, you can rotary-till the old plants to destroy them. If you have time, make sure the new plants get rooted down promptly, and then tuck mulch up around them to discourage weeds. This step takes a bit of handwork, but getting early runners rooted quickly and later runners pruned off will richly reward you with larger berries the following year. It will then be easy to pick a quart of big berries in a hurry, and win back the time you now spent hand-pruning and rooting.

In the fall of a strawberry bed's first year, cover it with straw *after* freeze-up. This lessens alternate freezing and thawing over winter and early spring, and so lessens frost-heaving. In spring, keep the straw over the bed for as long as possible without hurting the plants underneath. The longer you can keep them from starting to grow again, the later will be their blossoming time, and therefore the less chance of frost damage to the blooms. When the bed must be uncovered, rake the straw gingerly to the edges, leaving as much straw as possible among the plants. The plants will grow rapidly up over the straw, and your berries will stay clean of rain-splattered mud.

Buy the brightest straw you can find. Straw that has been rained on has lost some of its nutrient content, especially potassium, along with its luster. I have tried growing strawberries in leaf mulch, but straw always produces a better crop.

A strawberry mulch-bed has a three-year life span, the way I do it. This spring's new plants are next year's main crop. The main-crop plants usually are worth keeping for another year. Then mow them off after harvest, and bury them under leaf mulch. This bed then becomes a good place to set out late cabbage or broccoli plants.

### Tomato Beds

The first crop I grow when converting a conventional garden plot into a mulch bed is tomatoes. Tomatoes respond extremely well to mulch-bed gardening. Since the plants are usually about eight inches tall when I set them out, it is easy to spread the mulch around them thickly enough to thwart weeds, without inadvertently covering the tomato plants. Tomatoes stay clean on the mulch and do not need to be staked. As a bonus, blossom-end rot is less common in mulched tomatoes.

From August on, if not earlier, the plants grow so thick over the mulch that all potential weed growth is shaded out. Even during the following spring, weed growth is sparse, except for the seedling tomatoes from the previous year's huge surplus crop that I didn't get entirely cleaned up. Chickens allowed into the bed after the first hard frost will clean up some of these fruits and seeds, along with bug eggs, and, while searching for earthworms, will scratch and scatter the old mulch around so the ground freezes better over winter.

### Tree-Starting Beds

Mulch beds are an ideal place to plant tree seeds. Just stick them in the mulch. This method works well with fruit trees: Stick a whole rotten apple in the mulch, and save the most vigorous seedling that comes up. With all fruit seeds, but especially peach, it is good to let the seeds soak or stew and ferment in their juices for a few days before planting. (This is why the apple and pear seeds in pomace, left over from making cider, sprout so well.)

Many tree seeds, raked up in yard leaves (acorns and maple seeds, especially) sprout and grow in the leaf mulch without any help from you. You can dig them up for use elsewhere in landscaping, or to start a tree grove. Seeds carried in bird droppings that fall on the mulch bed also sprout and grow easily. It is not good to grow mulberry trees close to mulch beds, because in a few years you will be amazed at the crop of little mulberries coming up among your cabbages. And mulberry seedlings are almost impossible to pull out by hand, even when they are little.

Mulch-bed gardening can create an almost totally self-sustaining food system that can be operated with muscle power and hand tools. Mulch beds are best for small gardens, but since a modest plot in this hardly-ever-tilled style can produce two and a half times as much food as a conventional garden of the same size (because of close spacing and succession planting), it is not really small.

# CHAPTER 5

# THE HARDLY-EVER-TILLED GARDEN: POTTED PLANTS FOR THE MULCH BED

Mulch-bed gardening is more practical for setting out potted plants than for direct-seeding. Starting plants under cover presents the possibility of a food production system that is almost as protected from the vicissitudes of nature as greenhouse production, but a whole lot cheaper. Starting plants in an artificial environment means that you are much less at the mercy of nature's whim. You don't need to worry about rain on that precise day or weekend when you plan to put in the garden. Nor do you need to rush the season by tilling soil that is not really dry yet. You start your seeds indoors or outdoors under glass, rain or shine. Then you can set plants out when the garden soil is ready and when you have the time. While you are waiting for that perfect moment, plants under glass in the early and most fragile stage of growth are protected from adverse weather, bugs, moles, rabbits, and small children.

There is another advantage. When you start plants in pots, you can make nearly every seed count, so you do not need to buy as many. In the ideal soil of the potting mix, nearly every seed will come up.

What is often overlooked is that starting plants in pots or flats can be just as practical for fall gardens as for spring gardens. Often, direct-seeding in the garden in late summer for fall crops is difficult because the soil is too dry to support healthy germination. Instead, you can start seeds in pots, and easily supply the water necessary to get them off to a good start. When rain does come, you can set the plants out in the garden, and they will be already on their way.

## Getting Started

The best guide I've found for starting plants in relatively large quantities is Eliot Coleman's *The New Organic Grower* (Chelsea Green, 1995). He even tells you how to start vegetables that are normally direct-seeded, such as corn, peas, beans, lettuce, beets, and radishes. Coleman points out that planting several seeds per pot greatly decreases the work of setting out a planting of these kinds of vegetables. Also, for mulch-bed gardening, multiply-seeded pots can be spaced somewhat farther apart in the mulch bed than single seeds in a tilled row, which makes for easier mulching between plants, while the total number of plants is approximately the same.

The downside to starting plants under glass is that there is very little margin for error. Getting potting-soil mixes to heat up in the cold spring for proper germination is more difficult than putting seeds in the ground later and relying on Father Sun and Mother Earth. The environment under glass—whether it be a greenhouse, a hotbed, a cold frame, or even a south window in your house—tends to be either too cold at night or too hot during the day. Even in cold weather, the temperature in a little greenhouse can rocket to over 100 degrees Fahrenheit in half an hour once the sun comes out. Overheating will kill plants if it lasts long enough, or will encourage a white mold that in turn kills plants. As the old books all say, you must get the glass off the grow-frames in a hurry when the sun comes out, and you must keep that potting soil moist but not oversaturated.

Many gardeners therefore find it more practical to buy their plants from a nursery greenhouse—that's why the bedding-plant industry is so big, and growing bigger. You can plant seedlings from the typical little greenhouse pots directly into your garden, as most gardeners do, but this is not the best way. Plants in small pots (two inches or less) are often already rootbound and not well hardened off when you buy them. Transfer them into larger containers: the bottom half of a half-gallon milk carton, or similar-sized container, is about the right size: one-quart (or larger) cottage-cheese containers work well, too. Be sure to cut a few holes in the bottoms of whatever containers you use.

Once the little plants are growing well in these larger containers, and have hardened off better in a protected place outdoors, they can be transplanted to the garden with no setback or wilting to speak of. (My neighbors, the Riggles, use a little cart to temporarily hold these replanted transplants. They wheel the cart in and out of their shed to protect the plants at night and during storms, and to make the most of a sunny protected place outside during the day.) In the larger containers, you can keep plants into June (here in northern Ohio) before they have to be set out. Small plants purchased (usually on sale) at nurseries late in the spring can be transferred to larger pots and held through July or longer before setting them out.

But if you want to grow varieties not available from the nursery, or you are growing a large enough quantity of plants to justify the cost of starting your own, or if you want to avoid the possibility of importing pests or weed seeds from the nursery, or if you just enjoy raising your own potted plants, modern and traditional plant-starting aids exist today in many-splendored variety.

The most essential of these modern aids is the electric propagation mat, to provide heat under the pots or flats of seedlings. Even if you start plants in your warm house, you will find that supplementary bottom heat gives better results. Because these mats are sort of expensive ($50 is the norm as I write), we have used heat cables, a box with a lightbulb inside, and even a string of Christmas tree lights for bottom heat. My wife has also used an electric heating pad, first slipping a plastic covering over it.

Also available now are thermostatically controlled, automatic vent-openers for even the smallest greenhouses and cold frames. You can get along without them, and I do, but because of the volatile rise and fall of temperature in these structures on early spring days, automatic vents are very, very handy. Automatic capillary watering devices for trays of started plants are very, very handy, too, especially if you have to be away for a few days.

To round out the picture, you can also buy supplemental growing lights, premixed potting soils, special fertilizers, and a vast selection of transplant pots. Scores of catalogs cater to this trade. I haven't bought many of these planting aids, because I mix my own potting soils and have learned how to start plants outdoors under glass rather than in the house. So I don't need electric growing lights. But many of these devices are helpful, if you feel you can afford them.

I am a tightwad about greenhouses. For me, a greenhouse heated with some sort of fossil fuel is a luxury, like a swimming pool, and I must seek substitutes that I can afford. Gardeners looking for an economical way to own a small greenhouse might build it against their homes, in such a way as to take advantage of the home heating system. Even then, it will be practical to use some artificial heat under your trays of transplants.

Transplants started on a windowsill often grow too leggy, even with a supplemental fluorescent bulb positioned close above them. Kamyar Enshayan, an agricultural engineer and my favorite environmental gadfly, places a piece of cardboard faced with aluminum foil on the room side behind his window transplants, so that the sunlight reflects off the foil and back at the plants. "They grow nice and stout that way," he says.

A drawback to plants grown in supplementally heated greenhouses, as well as house windows, is that plants so grown need to be hardened off before transplanting to the open garden. Hardening off is not difficult exactly, but it can be a critical factor that many beginning gardeners are not properly warned about. Plants, tender from growing inside, need to get used to ("hardened" against) the scorching sunlight and chilly nights outdoors. We put young potted plants out only for an hour the first few times, and then only with some kind of old screen over them to filter the full effects of the sun.

Small, portable greenhouses are now available, such as the Green Mountain Sunshed sold by Gardener's Supply. These structures have solar panels on one side, with the rest of the little building framed in wood. This design allows you to insulate the building above and below the panels, and on the other walls, which makes the structure much easier to keep warm than a complete greenhouse. You can then get by without supplemental heat, other than warming pads under the trays, if you don't try to start plants too early in the year. If you do use a supplemental stove, such as a kerosene heater or a tiny woodstove, you will use less fuel than in a full-glass greenhouse.

## The Pit Greenhouse

If you can't afford to buy a passive solar greenhouse outright, you can build your own. Jan Dawson and Andy Reinhart, who live not far from us and whom I consider to be worthy successors to Helen and Scott Nearing, recently built an adaptation of the old pit solar hothouse against the south wall of their barn. With his little tractor and front-end loader, Andy scooped out a pit measuring about nine by sixteen feet. He and Jan then built the three sides of the structure out of wood, up to about waist-high at ground level. They used black locust for all the parts in contact with the ground, since this wood hardly rots at all, and white oak for the rest of the pit walls. For framing the upper part of the structure, they used black walnut, which is also very rot-resistant, and easier to nail than white oak. (Black walnut sounds expensive, but medium-grade boards from a country lumber mill are no more expensive than white oak.) "We felt more comfortable working with wood than with masonry," said Jan, "and we had access to the wood at a lower price."

Then Andy pushed the soil excavated from the pit back up against the walls, forming an insulating berm of earth about four feet high and equally thick. They roofed the structure with clear polycarbonate plastic panels. This material stays clear, but it is very hard, so holes for nails must be drilled through it. Entry to the hothouse is by way of the barn; a stair descends about three feet to the pit floor, from which position the earthen berm outside is about at eye level.

We visited Jan and Andy (they call their garden farm business "Jandy's") on a day in early March when they were busy boiling maple sap from about forty trees on their little spread. They sell the syrup at their farmer's market booth in Columbus, Ohio, along with vegetables and their mainstays: gourds and dried flowers (see chapter 2). Their sap boiler is typical Jandy ingenuity, an ancient barrel stove from which a welder cut the top side so that it would admit the sap pans, which came from a dump. As boiling progresses, Andy dips the sap from one pan to another, so that new sap is continuously starting in the first pan while finished syrup taken off the third. The sugarhouse is almost entirely glass (recycled windows) and faces south, because Andy at first thought he might use it as a greenhouse to take advantage of the heat from boiling off the sap. But this idea didn't turn out to be too practical, since their sap season doesn't last long enough (though it is still an idea worth thinking about).

During a break in the boiling process, we took a look at their new pit hothouse. Because we had recently suffered frigid weather, I was surprised at the vigor of the onion seedlings, which had been started in the house in February, moved to the greenhouse before that dip in the weather, and now stood approximately five inches tall. "They got yellow and droopy, but pulled out of it when warmer weather returned," said Andy. "We had no supplemental heat, but did stack plastic jugs of water around them. The water, warmed during the day, plus blankets over the flats, kept the plants from freezing." Lettuce and cole vegetables were doing quite well also, and eight tomato plants on the bench were already eight inches tall. "We wanted only a solar-heated greenhouse," said Andy. "A fuel-heated, year-round greenhouse seems to us to defeat the purpose of environmental gardening." But in early April, they were forced to use a kerosene heater during a record-breaking cold snap.

The structure cost Jandy's $647 out of pocket: gravel, $50; drain tile (some of it scavenged), $20; black locusts for posts and oak for pit walls, $115; walnut for framing, $70; glazing, $346; windows (scavenged); flashing, $16; screws, nails, and other materials, $30. With the outside temperature around 50 degrees Fahrenheit on the sunny day when we were there, the inside temperature had soared to over 90 degrees, and Jan had opened windows to allow for some air circulation. A thermometer that registers highs and lows as well as present temperature indicated that the previous night's reading had reached about 40 degrees Fahrenheit inside while the mercury had dropped to below freezing outside.

Jan and Andy have only one criticism of their solar greenhouse: They wish it were bigger. "The negative thing is that we can't use it for growing plants in summer," says Jan. "It just stays too hot in there for most plants, no matter how much air circulation we generate." They may try to solve the problem by adding some sort of shade or covering.

## Hotbeds and Cold Frames

The traditional hotbed is the poor folks' greenhouse. It can be managed to avoid some of the problems of passive solar greenhouses. For one thing, it is easier to keep warm in cold weather, and in warm weather, the top glass (or plastic) can be taken off completely to prevent overheating. The heart of the hotbed is a pit two and a half feet deep, with a frame above and around it at ground level, usually 6- by 6-feet square to allow covering by two standard 3- by 6-foot glass sashes. Of course, any manageable size for the hotbed will do, depending on the size of your sashes. (Many gardeners use discarded windows from old houses for sashes.) Old books insist that the frame should be six inches higher at the back than in front, so that the glass slants six inches over the full width of six feet. This angle is supposed to allow the glass to refract the sunlight to the plants most efficiently and, in any event, helps shed water.

Outside the hotbed, the gardener makes a compost heap—traditionally of horse manure, because it heats easily, or alternate six-inch (approximately) layers of horse manure and leaves—starting about a month before the hotbed is to be planted. The compost goes through its first heat, is thrown together again (more on composting later in this chapter), and as it reaches its peak temperature (160 degrees Fahrenheit) in its second heat, it is forked into the hotbed pit, and then covered with six inches of soil. Seeds are then planted, very shallow. The heat of the compost prompts germination, and the rising ammonia feeds the plant roots without harming the leaves.

Because there is limited air space in a hotbed, maintaining proper temperature is crucial on sunny days. The temperature can rise quickly to well over 100 degrees Fahrenheit and kill seedlings, either directly or by encouraging harmful molds. No matter how cold the outside air, the glass sashes have to be at least partially opened on sunny days, and even on partly cloudy days. Thermostatically controlled vent-openers can relieve this worry. On the other hand, on cold nights like almost every early spring night around here, an old blanket or other insulating cover should be placed over the hotbed.

Plants usually are dug up out of the hotbed for transplanting into the garden after danger of frost has passed. However, in many commercial enterprises a century ago, plants were allowed to grow out to market maturity right there in the frame. A whole acre of hotbeds was not uncommon.

Cold frames basically are hotbeds without the heat: a hotbed used without supplemental heat becomes a cold frame. I think that cold frames are eminently practical for all gardeners, while I have my doubts about hotbeds. I can start any spring garden crop from seed in a cold frame, and gain two weeks compared to planting it in the garden. In a hotbed, my experience is that most of the time, I scarcely gain another week over the same crop in a cold frame. Is lettuce one week earlier worth all the work of a hotbed? Later in the season, cold frames really show their worth in protecting August-planted lettuce and cole crops into early winter, even in northern Ohio.

## The Hothut

I don't know when the idea first crept into my mind, but I know when it jumped up out of the bushes of my brain and shouted, "Eureka!" I was watching on television (bless me, Father, for I have sinned) a gardening video based on that delightful book, *The 3,000 Mile Garden* (Penguin, 1997), in which two gardeners, Leslie Land in New England and Roger Philips in Old England, exchange letters about their gardening experiences through the year. In the segment I was watching, Mr. Philips was doing something very strange. He was burying a perfectly good ham in a pile of leaves. He said, to my amazement, that the ham baked nicely (it had actually been preboiled a little, he admitted) in the heat generated by the composting yard waste. Hmmmmm.

In previous years, I had argued against making compost piles. I don't do work that nature will do for me. Why endure heap big trouble making big trouble heaps?

But I had failed to consider the added fertility that results (mysteriously to me, but read on) from properly made compost, as well as the imaginative uses to which the heat of composting can be put. The baked ham indicated that there were any number of imaginative things to do with the heat of composting. Then I read a report by Larry Bass and T. E. Bilderback of the North Carolina Cooperative Extension Service (published in *American Small Farm,* April 1996) about how growers in the Netherlands were making compost in their greenhouses to take advantage of both the heat *and* the carbon dioxide generated in the composting process. Plants "consume" carbon dioxide. The growers had even found a way to pump the ammonia, which is also produced during composting and which can be harmful to plant leaves, to the plant roots, which use it for fertilizer. Could I do something similar but cheap enough for a backyard tightwad?

I decided to build what I called a hothut. In essence, I enclosed a compost heap with concrete blocks and put a wooden frame with a glass top over it. My theory was that the heat of the composting would germinate seeds earlier than in the garden and keep the plants growing during early-spring cold spells without recourse to electric propagating mats. (Whether the hothut can double as an oven to bake hams in, I can't yet say.) Also, the compost would give off carbon dioxide, enhancing plant growth. Experience showed me that setting the flats directly on top of the compost worked better than setting them on a platform above the pile

After the need for supplemental heat passed, my hothut became a tall cold frame, at which I could work as at a bench in the greenhouse to start seeds for succession planting until fall, relieving my back and knees from bending over and crawling around a conventionally low cold frame. The finished compost became potting soil and, still in the hothut, could serve as a "worm barn" for the rest of the year.

I made my hothut out of standard concrete blocks that cost me about $60 in actual cash outlay ($1.03 each). Shortly afterwards, I found a source of old blocks that would have cost me next to nothing. Such is life. At least, the wooden grow-frame that sits on top of the cement blocks came from our own lumber, and we got the glass out of an old building for free from a home remodeler. I also used some leftover bricks, from building our house, in the walls of the hothut.

The width and length of a hothut can be any dimension, depending on the maximum number of transplant pots you need to grow at any given time, or how much compost you wish to make at one time. Four square feet of space was ample for me. If I ever need more room, I can always tear down one wall and add to the size of the hothut because the concrete blocks are stacked dry.

Dry-stacking the blocks meant that the first layer had to be reasonably level, so that all the layers above it would also stack up level. (I didn't have the wiggle room that mortar would have given me.) I set my first layer in the ground only enough to achieve that levelness, and I didn't bother to make a footer under the walls. They therefore may become slightly crooked as the ground freezes and thaws over the years, but they can be easily realigned or relaid entirely. So far, no problem.

For a compost heap to heat up dependably, it should be about five feet tall, say the books. I built my bin only four feet tall, and then heaped the compost up to nearly five feet, knowing that it would subside below the frame level as it heated.

I designed the frame for the glass so that the glass would slant five or six inches higher from front to back. Height between the glass and the plants should be at least eight inches in front, which means that at the rear, the glass will sit about a foot above the plant trays. With that much room, few seedlings will reach the glass before they are set out in the garden. And since the glass is slanted, I can move the plants to the back as they grow and keep the younger ones in front.

I made the frame for the glass out of regular inch-thick red-oak boards, although because of the moist warm air coming off the compost, a more rot-resistant wood such as white oak, redwood, or black walnut would have been better. I used what I had. The frame fits inside the top layer of blocks and rests on the edges of the next layer. I allowed this second layer of blocks to protrude in from the walls, just enough to hold the frame in position.

In the bottom layer of blocks at ground level, I laid one block on its side in each of two opposing walls, so that the holes in the blocks would allow outside air in to the bottom of the compost heap. On the floor of the bin, I laid two pieces of perforated plastic drainpipe (4-inch diameter), extending from the concrete block holes in one wall to the concrete-block holes in the opposite wall, to increase air circulation under the pile.

Two more lengths of this drainpipe I positioned vertically inside the bin, toward the middle, about a foot and half apart. These standpipes direct hot air from the middle of the compost heap directly up to the plants. On a cold day in March or April, I can hold my hand over the vents and feel the hot air gushing out. To hold the standpipes in place, I simply stuck two wooden stakes in the ground and slipped the pipes over them.

I didn't fasten down the wooden top frame (which can't go anywhere, hemmed in by the blocks) so that I can easily lift it out if necessary. The two glass panes, each about two by four feet, also sit loose on the frame, but strips of wood along the outer front and rear edge of the frame form lips that keep the glass from sliding off. The panes can be slid open sideways, however, or taken off completely. (If you cut glass to fit your grow-frame, burnish the edges a little with a file. The glass-cutter leaves an extremely sharp edge on the glass. In hindsight, I recommend getting clear, rigid plastic material for a covering, not glass.)

I learned quickly that a thermometer in the hothut was necessary for keeping close tabs on the temperature. At over 85 degrees Fahrenheit, you will want to get the glass panes propped open to keep things from getting too hot and moist inside. Try not to let the temperature rise above 90–100 degrees Fahrenheit after the plants have come up. This takes some experience, as the temperature in my hothut will quickly clear 100 degrees when the sun is shining, even if the outside temperature is only 50 degrees. I've had to experiment continuously to find out how far to open the glass in order to keep the inside temperature at about 85 degrees. When the outside temperature rises above 60 degrees and the sun is shining, it is best to remove the glass completely. Plants will die if the heat inside soars over 120 degrees. Even on cloudy, cool days, the glass will have to stay partially open, and if the outside temperature is above

55 degrees, the glass needs to be more than half open to keep the inside temperature around 85 degrees. (For growing summer transplants in a hothut, you should definitely have some screen covers on hand to take the place of the glass. The main reason is not to reduce sun glare, although that is helpful, but because several insect pests—especially cabbage worms and those dratted flea beetles—will demolish little seedlings just coming up. Flea beetles are not accustomed to finding delectable young leaves in August, and they think an unscreened hothut is heaven.)

I was determined to start the seeds with only the heat of composting. But even with a blanket over the hothut glass, a series of nights with temperatures in the single digits kept the hothut too cold for reliable germination. I then insulated the inside of the concrete-block walls with corrugated cardboard: This helped, but did not solve the problem completely until the overnight weather warmed up to above 25 degrees Fahrenheit.

I'm convinced that it hardly pays in northern Ohio to start plants much before the first day of spring. Research, most recently by Scott Nesmith at the University of Georgia, shows that starting seeds of melons, squash, and cucumbers indoors means earlier harvest, but whether you start them two weeks or two months early, the yield is about the same. My experience is that this is true of tomatoes, peppers, and eggplants, too. Only onions are an exception; they need a very early start in northern Ohio if you want to grow them as big as softballs. The better onion alternative is to order early transplants by the bunch from Texas. On the other hand, you don't really need softball-sized onions, except for bragging.

After working with concrete blocks, I'm sure that straw or hay bales would make a better and certainly cheaper hothut. They would provide a lot more insulation to keep the air warm in the hothut. Since it would take about five minutes to build a straw-bale hothut, and since a dozen straw bales should cost hardly $20, and since you could then use the old bales for mulch, building a new one every year would not be a problem.

Of course, you also could make a hothut entirely of wood, with a door in the side for easier removal of the compost. You could possibly make one out of steel barrels, if you insulated it. Turn your own innovative mind loose to experiment.

If you want a hothut without messing with compost, that is easily accomplished. A hundred years ago, such a structure was called a plant incubator. Envisage it as a little cabinet measuring two feet per side, with a door in front but no top. In place of a top was a piece of sheet metal, the same width as the inside of the cabinet, but with the other two edges a little longer so they could be bent at a 90-degree angle and nailed to the inside top of the cabinet. Above the cabinet was secured a rectangular heat chamber made of 1- by 6-inch boards, six feet long and two feet wide, nailed and braced together to make a frame. The bottom was boarded over, except where the center of the frame sat over the top of the cabinet and its sheet metal heating diaphragm. A kerosene lamp was placed in the cabinet, and its heat rose to the sheet-metal which acted as a radiator, spreading the heat more evenly through the heat chamber above.

The top of the heat chamber was open, but flats of plants placed on it formed a cover so that no heat could escape, except up through the flats. Glass sashes covered the flats when necessary. In the old days, asbestos paper was used as insulation in the lamp chamber and the heating chamber. (Any kind of cheap, nonflammable insulation would do as a modern substitute, although there is little danger of fire.) The lamp was positioned so that the top of the glass chimney was four inches from the sheet metal above it.

So effective were these little incubators that often a second layer of flats could be stacked above the first, starting as many as nine hundred plants at once. Needless to say, the device should set in a sunny, wind-protected place.

I imagine that you could make a plant incubator in other ways, perhaps out of a metal barrel. A kerosene lamp would still be as cheap a source of heat today as it was years ago, and is still available (see especially the catalog from Lehman's Hardware, Kidron, Ohio 44636). But a light-bulb would work okay, too, and a heat bulb definitely would.

## Making Compost

Obviously, the success of the hothut depends on the success of the composting process. Even if starting plants in its heat is not your goal, making good compost surely should be. Compost in the potting soil is also the key to successful transplants. It helps prevent damping-off disease and other fungal problems.

Large piles of carbonaecous materials heat up fast and fairly easily, but to get a *small* compost pile to stand and deliver on schedule is not press-the-button automatic. Composting involves the care and feeding of microscopic animals and plants, and they can be as perverse as mules. Composting is farming, not manufacturing.

For hotbeds, oldtimers all insist that horse manure is best. Cow manure is too "cold" and won't heat up fast, they say. So I have obediently used horse manure as the main ingredient in my hothut compost bin, and have not regretted it.

In the hothut, speedy compost was not my goal however; warmth that lasted six weeks was. It is inconvenient to turn the compost often to hasten breakdown in a hothut anyway, because of the trays of plants on top of the heap. I turned mine only once about a month after I built the heap, and then only partially—just enough to get a little rise in temperature again.

The two key factors in successful composting are the moisture and texture of the material. As you layer the ingredients into your pile, water them only *if* they are dry. According to Albert Howard, the guru of composting (see chapter 1), and everybody since then, the right moisture content of composting materials is that of a wet sponge squeezed out. Horse manure fresh from the stable does not need added water, especially in the concrete-block bin, which reduces evaporation from the outside of the heap.

Chopping or grinding the materials greatly improves your success as a composter, but here again, the main effect is acceleration of the process. So for the simple purpose of keeping plants warm in the hothut, fine grinding is not so crucial. The texture of horse manure is usually okay as it comes from the stable, because it does not cake. But with cakey manure, I simply shake it apart as I put it in the hothut. I "rake" my leaves in the fall with the mower, passing over them three times as I mow-blow them into windrows. This shreds them nicely for composting purposes. You can run your mower over hay or straw chunks to chop them more finely if necessary. Table scraps I would add in very thin layers to the compost heap, though as a matter of fact we feed ours to the chickens. If you can figure out a way of catching food scraps after they go through your garbage disposal, they would make an ideal addition to your compost heap, but only in very thin layers between more fibrous materials. In the absence of rich nitrogenous material of natural origin, a sprinkling of chemical fertilizer on every other layer or so will aid in heating up the pile. But of course this is organic heresy, on a par with rooting for the Cleveland Indians if you live in Cincinnati.

Here is a sample of a good layered mix of composting materials that works for me:

- 6 inches of mower-chopped leaves
- 8 inches of horse manure (preferably with only a little or no bedding)
- 1 inch of topsoil (or aged compost if you have it)
- A sprinkling of wood ashes or limestone (even an inch is too much: it might cake into a layer that will inhibit air circulation)

Repeat this layering or a similar one until the pile is about four to five feet high.

The intensity and duration of heat in the compost pile is the crucial question for plant protection. Here's what the patron saint of composting, Albert Howard, has to say: "A very high temperature—149 degrees Fahrenheit—is established at the outset [by which he means in a few days] which continues with a moderate downward gradient to 86 degrees Fahrenheit at the end of ninety days." During that time, his instruction is to turn the pile after the first three weeks, and then again two to three weeks later. "Before each turn, a definite slowing down in the fermentation takes place: this is accompanied by a fall in temperature." I mention this only so you know. If you do have a temperature fall below 80 degrees Fahrenheit, in the first six weeks, which is highly unlikely with a good layered mixture containing horse manure, you would want to get in there and turn the pile a little, forking the less decomposed material from the outside of the pile into the middle, and from the middle to the outside.

And how good is that compost when it is mature? Again I quote Howard: "Soon after the second turn, the ripening process begins. It is during this period that the fixation of atmospheric nitrogen takes place. Under favorable circumstances *as much as 25 percent* of additional free nitrogen may be secured from the atmosphere [italics mine]." That's what gardeners are referring to when they speak of the magical power of compost.

I love the hothut idea because it allows me to make at least four products with one effort: heat, transplants, mulch, and fertilizer. That's the kind of efficiency I survive on. Every act of farming must accomplish several goals; everything I write must be usable in more than one way.

## Plant Pots and Soil Blocks

Gardeners love to argue about the advantages and disadvantages of different kinds of plant pots. Pots made of decomposable materials that are put into the soil along with the plant prevent root disturbance. But these pots don't usually decompose as fast as they should, so there is some slight blockage of roots growing out into the ground. On the other hand, tiny root hairs are broken or torn loose from soil when plants are removed from pots. This is less a problem with plants that regrow roots quickly, such as tomatoes and onions, and more a problem with plants that don't, such as corn. In impermeable pots, roots wrap around themselves looking for a place to get out, and such plants sulk a little after being transplanted. Whether it is cheaper to use disposable pots or slightly more expensive reusable ones, I don't know, since this gets into the debate about the cost of generating more trash rather than less. Probably those little wooden contrivances that make pots out of waste paper are the "best" in environmental terms, and most garden catalogs sell them. Jan Dawson makes paper pots by hand, no gadget needed.

Some gardeners prefer pots that are shaped like upside-down pyramids. The theory is that that the plant and root clump will slide out easily, and this will not disturb the roots as much. Other people point out that a standard cylindrical or cubic pot provides more room for root development than the inverted pyramids do, and that the plants slide out of it well enough anyway. All pots work okay in my experience. What you really need to worry about is sufficient moisture at transplanting time.

Following Coleman's *The New Organic Grower,* I tried using soil blocks this year and liked them too. No pot is involved at all, just compressed soil, compost, and peat. For most home gardeners, it is easy enough to accumulate a bunch of reusable plastic pots over the years, and they suffice for the smaller garden. We also use milk cartons and cottage-cheese containers. But soil blocks are worthwhile when you want to start a relatively large quantity of plants, especially if you intend to grow pots of crops you normally direct-seed. Soil blocks will pay for themselves quickly in this situation. My soil-block maker makes four 2-inch cube blocks at a time and costs $25. Machines that make smaller and larger blocks are also available. I would prefer a 3-incher for multiplanting three to four seeds of corn or peas per pot, but for single seeding, the 2-incher is fine. Plants in 2-inch blocks can be transplanted into larger pots for better results, but also can be set directly into the garden.

The soil-block maker compresses potting soil into a cube that, with the right mix of materials and the right moisture, will keep intact until it is set into the garden. The block maker puts a little indentation in the top of the cube for the seed. Professionals make soil blocks by plunging the block maker into an appropriate pile of wet potting soil on a bench, forcing the soil into the square metal compartments. The gardener lifts and twists the block maker deftly to break the sticky seal between the soil in the block forms and the soil in the pile, and then deposits the blocks in a plant tray by pushing down on a plunger. This is all accomplished in one swift motion. Since I hardly ever make more than thirty pots at a sitting, I use a cruder, slower method. I hold the block maker upside-down in my left hand over the bucket of wet soil mix, and gob the block forms full of soil with my right hand, pressing the soil in firmly and smoothing it off with the palm of my hand. Then I hold the block maker over a tray, and with the plunger push the four blocks out. They often don't want to come all the way out until I shake the block maker gently. Sloshing the block maker in water between refills allows the blocks to slide out easier.

Preparing the potting soil itself is fun. I guess I never got to make enough mud pies when I was a child. You can experiment with all sorts of materials in all sorts of mixtures, but first follow the recipes known to work, such as the one that comes with my block maker: 1 part bagged topsoil, 1 part sphagnum peat, 1 part moss peat, ½ part vermiculite, ¾ part water. The directions suggest a 2-quart saucepan as a measuring device. A small bucket works well for larger amounts.

Being contrary, I make up my own mixture: composted chicken manure, sphagnum peat, and my own topsoil in about equal amounts. I keep edging toward more compost and less topsoil, because there are fewer weed seeds in the compost. A little lime helps too. I mix the ingredients together thoroughly and then add water. I add just enough water until the mix is thoroughly wet, but not runny.

I hesitate to give specific recipes for soil-block potting mixes, since if you use homemade ingredients, they will likely not have the same physical or chemical makeup as mine, and so will not give the same results. Experiment and come up with your own measures. Precision about various materials does not seem to be crucial. Experimentation is easy (and fun) since you can just keep pressing out soil blocks till you get the mix that brings you the best results. If you waste some blocks, you have not lost money; you can pulverize them and use them in other mixes. You should be able to handle the blocks right out of the block maker, but it is best to place them from the block maker directly into a plant tray so you don't have to handle them immediately. A spatula is handy for moving them from the tray to the garden, or from one tray to another.

Use as much compost in your mix as the soil blocks will take without crumbling. Harry Hoitink, a plant pathologist at Ohio State, is internationally famous for proving that compost in potting soils actually prevents many diseases, including the common damping-off disease. At his urging, I visited a large commercial nursery recently that sells container-grown and field-grown ornamentals. The nursery owner told me, quite excitedly, that using compost has reduced disease so effectively that he no longer needs fungicides on most crops. But to make it work, the compost needs to be fully mature and aged. Make some this year; stockpile it for use next year.

Trays to hold the soil blocks should have holes in them to let water through. Start out watering your blocks with a mister. An empty plastic spray bottle works perfectly. After the blocks are set from becoming moistened and then slightly drying a few times, you can use a sprinkling can, taking care not to deluge the blocks. (You might wash seeds out of the pots fairly easily.) Keep the blocks soaked for good germination. They can fool you; they may look moist enough, but be too dry. I now set soil blocks directly into the hothut compost—no trays—and this keeps them moist without frequent watering.

Plant your seeds, normally one per pot, in the little indentation on top of the soil block. If conditions are right for growth, one seed is enough; if not, two won't grow either. Occasionally, of course, a seed is not viable but better to miss a pot than waste a seed. You can always re-seed the empty pot. Only the slightest covering of compost, or nothing at all, is necessary over the seeds.

Sometimes, as discussed earlier, you will want to plant three or four seeds per pot. In multiplanting large seeds (such as corn, beans, and peas), I have found that a 2-inch block is not large enough. Use a 3-inch soil block or larger, and push the seeds into the block so that they aren't riding on top of one another. For smaller-seeded plants (beets and radishes especially), two or three seeds per 2-inch pot will grow fine. However, carrots will not develop well in little pots. The roots quickly get gnarled and stunted.

Fingering out seeds individually for planting in pots can be a pain when planting lots of trays. Several planting aids are available from catalogs to make this job easier. Another way is to put the seeds in a little saucer and use a baby spoon or doll spoon to dip them out. Then scrape excess seeds back into the saucer with a tiny screwdriver or similar tool. That way you know you have the right number in the spoon before putting them in the pot. You can also use a moist toothpick to pick up tiny seeds one at a time. Since I plant only about thirty soil blocks at a given time, I merely jostle a few seeds out of the packet into the palm of my hand. Then with my fingers, I move one (or whatever number I want) from the main pile in my hand and drop it (them) in the block.

It is important to say that in experimenting with a new idea, you should not expect perfect success the first time. In my second year with soil blocks and propagation by compost heat, I've had more success than the first time. There are tricks you can only learn by experience—like setting the soil blocks right down into the warm, moist compost of the hothut for quicker germination.

## CHAPTER 6

# FLOUR GARDENS AND
# PANCAKE PATCHES

While nutritionists are telling us that grains should form the greater part of our diet—the foundation of the food pyramid—grain gardening is the most neglected aspect of backyard food production. How can this be accounted for? Grains are easier to grow than vegetables. And threshing a bushel of wheat requires no more work than shelling a peck of peas.

I suspect the answer lies in tradition. Grain was part of the barnyard domain, not the kitchen garden. Fairly large amounts of corn, wheat, and oats were required for farm animals. Threshing whole fields was very laborious, so humans soon bent their ingenuity to making mechanical threshers. Grinding large amounts of grain into meal was also hard work, and so even before threshers, mechanical mills came into vogue. Gristmills were the first example of centralized agribusiness. Farmers hauled their grain to the mill because it was easier to grind large amounts that way, rather than by hand at home. And oh yes, a couple of sacks of flour for the Missus, too.

Since a bushel of wheat, for example, weighs in at fifty-eight to sixty pounds, it makes about that many loaves of whole-wheat bread. So today's family of four needs perhaps two or three bushels of grain to supply its flour for the year. This quantity is not a big deal to produce in the backyard and process in the kitchen. The Missus understood that in earlier times, I'm sure, but you can bet she was not going to make a point of it. She was overburdened already. As long as the Mister considered it his duty to supply her with flour and meal, that was fine with her.

Baking with flour dry, straight from the mill, may be the best agribusiness way, but it is not the best dietary way. Better for human digestion are foods made from *fermented* grains, say dieticians such as Sally Fallon, Pat Connolly, and Mary Enig, whose book *Nourishing Traditions* (Promotion Publishing, 1996) I refer to often in this book. (No, I do not have any business or personal connections with these people. I just agree with their point of view.)

Soaking whole grains overnight before using them, slightly ferments them, and greatly enhances their healthfulness, maintains the Fallon nutritional school of thought. All grains contain phytic acid, which blocks the absorption of calcium, phosphorus, iron, and especially zinc, leading to mineral deficiencies and bone loss. Soaking and fermenting whole grains allows lactobacilli and other helpful organisms to neutralize phytic acid. Soaking also neutralizes enzyme inhibitors and encourages the production of beneficial enzymes. It helps the body assimilate proteins from hard-to-digest gluten, too.

Soaking and fermenting grains, not to mention sprouting them, also expands tremendously the variety of food choices and tastes that you can derive from your garden: bulghur, cornbread, buckwheat crepes, sourdough whole-wheat bread, fried mush, and oatmeal porridge, to name a few. Nor is processing grains in these ways difficult or expensive on a small scale. "Breads, muffins, and pancakes that have been made with soaked whole-wheat or spelt flour need no baking powder to make them rise; and they are not characterized by the heaviness that can make whole grain products unpalatable," points out Fallon in her book. Almost all her recipes for whole-grain products call for soaking the grain or flour overnight before cooking or baking.

It amuses me no end to learn that we should be presoaking grains before eating them, because while society was abandoning that practice when I was a child on the farm, we continued to presoak grains for our hogs. It was my job to fill the barrel of "slop," as we called it, with water and ground corn and oats every evening for overnight soaking. It was not exactly an easy job to stir fifty-five gallons of slop until the water and feed had mixed to porridge-like consistency, but I didn't mind because of the pleasant smell of fermenting grain that issued from the barrel.

Technology makes kitchen processing of grains into flour and meal easy today. Soaking requires only a pan of water. And many models of electric or hand-cranked kitchen grinders are now available to mill the grains. And surprise, surprise, the Mister can actually operate these utensils as well as the Missus, and often is intrigued to do so, not to mention learning how to operate pasta cutters and bread machines and other gadgets that make centuries-old food practices easy and quick today. So more and more modern homes fill with the redolent aromas of the kitchen hearth of yesteryear.

Procuring good clean grains, let alone organic grains, is more difficult for urban families than processing them into baked goods at home. Commercially stored grain is treated with very strong pesticides to protect against weevils and fungal diseases. No harm results to breakfast-cereal eaters that I hear of, but it bothers me. (Fallon says to "throw away" all processed, boxed cereals.) Recently, a company that stores grain for one of the big cereal manufacturers was indicted by the FDA for using an unapproved chemical to fumigate grain. But then I read that the approved pesticide came from the same family of chemicals as the unapproved one. Hmmmmm.

If you buy rather than grow your own grain, the safest, surest way to get a clean supply is to know a farmer who will sell you a couple of bushels right out of the combine during harvest season. You may want to rinse such grain in water to rid it of possible harvest dust. (Use a colander; then spread the grain out on a clean sheet to dry right away so it doesn't mold.) As a young man in the Minnesota harvest fields, I often heard from old German farmers that only in modern times did housewives have to rely on yeast to make the dough rise well. In the days when wheat stalks were cut, bound into sheaves, and stood in shocks in the field for a month or more before threshing, the moisture from rain soaking into the shock would cause the wheat berries to begin to sprout just a wee bit; the sprouting process would then be arrested by the return of dry weather. Flour made from this sprouted wheat would rise well without yeast, my mentors said.

I took this claim to be folklore until I read a quote (in *Nourishing Traditions,* cited above) from Edward Howell, M.D., an enzyme specialist, extolling the health benefits of sprouted grains. He says that in the past, humans ate most of their grain in partially germinated form because the grain standing in sheaves and stacks in open fields often sprouted before it was brought into storage. That's not true of modern grain harvesting, where the grain is harvested directly from the stalk, and if not dry enough for large-scale storage, is run through a dryer. So maybe there's truth in the old folklore about baking bread from shocked grain being easier.

But a better way to get your own clean grain is to follow the advice of the Little Red Hen: Grow your own.

If a typical family today decided to produce annually 200 pounds of bread flour (1 pound per loaf of bread) and 50 pounds of cornmeal (½ pound per pan of cornbread), the amount of land needed would be minimal. For the wheat flour, figuring a yield of 50 bushels (about 300 pounds) of wheat per acre, you would need a plot approximately thirty feet by one hundred feet. For 50 pounds of cornmeal, at an average yield of 120 bushels per acre, you would need a plot roughly twenty-feet square. Yields could be much higher in both cases, and so less space might be required. Corn in optimum situations has yielded over 300 bushels per acre, and wheat over 100 bushels per acre. In other words, a whole lot of homes have more than enough lawn to convert to use for flour gardens and pancake patches.

Grain gardening fits in very well with vegetables and berries, especially in mulch-bed systems. The rotation of grain, vegetables, and berries effectively controls disease and weed pests. For example, dandelions can become a scourge in mulch beds, and not even an army of goldfinches gobbling dandelion seed and using the fluff for their nests can control the weed. A flock of sheep on your lawn will do the job, but this is not usually practical. So proceed in the following manner: Lightly till the dandelion-infested mulch bed with a rotary tiller, and plant corn in rows. Clean cultivate between the rows through the summer (details in the next section). Goodbye dandelions.

After the corn ears are harvested and the stalks removed (stalks make good animal forage), lightly till the soil surface and broadcast wheat (or winter rye, barley, spelt, triticale, or other winter grain) in September. Lightly till again to cover the seeds a wee bit. These overwintering grains will grow until frost, like a lawn, and then go dormant in late fall, greening up again in spring. While the wheat is still dormant in March, interseed a clover into it, again by broadcasting. Even just lying on top of the bare ground between the grain plants, the clover will germinate and grow along with the grain as warm weather arrives. Harvest the grain when ripe (see ahead in this chapter) and in late summer mow the clover, which by then will be growing vigorously along with weeds. The clippings can be fed to animals or allowed to rot down for mulch. The clover will regrow (but the weeds won't) until cold weather arrives. The next spring, the clover will come on strong. Mow it, cover it with leaves, and start your mulch-bed system again by transplanting tomatoes into the leaves as described in chapter 4.

## Backyard Corn

Corn is the easiest grain to grow in most parts of the United States. If you know how to grow sweet corn, you know how to grow any corn, because the culture is the same for all. Any corn will make meal too, even popcorn. Some gardeners plant more sweet corn and popcorn than they need, and use the surplus for meal. Sweet corn, parched, makes a good snack too, thrown into the popper with the popcorn. ('Silver Queen' makes good parched corn.) Sweet-corn meal is a tad soft for milling, but okay. Regular field corn, white or yellow, makes good meal. Our neighbors get old-fashioned, open-pollinated corn from us ('Reid Yellow Dent') because they think it makes the tastiest meal. Since we've never tried any other, we don't know any better. Some people prefer the old yellow flint corn, which is very hard. Others like blue corn from the Southwest. R. H. Shumway Seedsman (P.O. Box 1, Graniteville, South Carolina 29829) is one mail-order source for all kinds of field-corn seed, including some of the old fashioned, open-pollinated varieties ('Reid Yellow Dent', 'Lancaster Surecrop', 'Truckers Favorite', and 'Hickory King', to name a few).

I've never tasted cornmeal that wasn't good, as long as it was fresh. The best comes from naturally dried corn, stored as earcorn rather than shelled. Shell only as you need it. That's good advice for popcorn, too.

### Planting and Cultivation

I usually grow corn of all kinds in rows in the customary manner, following the directions that come with the specific variety I am planting. I cultivate weeds between the rows with a tiller, starting as soon as the corn comes up. At the second cultivation, when the corn is about three inches tall, I roll some of the loose dirt from the cultivation over between the plants in the row to bury weeds trying to grow there. This is a fairly easy maneuver, and a lot faster than trying to hoe between the plants. I straddle the row and sort of shuffle along, dragging dirt over the weeds in the row with my feet. It is essential that the weeds not be allowed to grow much more than an inch, or they become too tall to bury easily by shuffling.

I may cultivate a third and even a fourth time, quitting when the corn gets above a foot high because by that time, the tiller blades may harm the corn roots spreading out from the plants. Once the corn is knee-high, it shades out most weed growth.

### Harvesting and Storage

Harvest corn for roasting to suit your taste. We like it a little on the tender green side. All sweet corn that I have ever examined in supermarkets was picked too late from the stalk for our tastes. In addition, commercial corn, shipped from afar, is also usually two days or more from the field, which further dulls its taste. I often wonder why corn on the cob continues to be so popular when what most people take home from the store is nearly inedible. The new corns with higher sugar content make up some of the lack of freshness, but not much.

To eat corn fresh from the garden, husk the ears, boil them in a little water for about three minutes, butter, and eat. For a change of taste, charcoal-broil corn in the husk over an outdoor grill. Some people wrap the husk with wet newspaper before grilling; the newspaper protects the kernels from getting burned better than the green husks alone.

Popcorn kernels should be hard and dry on the ears before harvesting. We leave the husks on, but strip them back off the ears and tie the husks to wires strung across the garage in a way that makes it difficult for mice to get at it. When we want to pop corn, we take down a couple of ears and shell them. Stored in a dry, unheated garage, our popcorn still pops well four years later. In fact, I don't know how long it will store this way, because we've never kept it any longer than that.

Field corn to be used for meal can be allowed to hang on the stalk until the kernels are deeply dented on top and feel quite dry and hard. But even in October, the corn will probably not be as dry as it feels, and so can be stored safely only in an airy crib that measures no more than four feet wide so air can penetrate to the middle. (The length of the crib doesn't matter.) If stored in a tight barrel, the corn will probably mold. Your crib can be made of wood with slatted walls and roof enough to keep out rain. Any snow that blows in through the slats will not harm the corn. Alternately, you can use a roll of chicken-wire fence for a crib, or even a ring of snow fence. Here again, the diameter should not be more than four feet to allow for good air penetration.

If you lack a suitable crib, leave the ears on the plants until the stalks have started to die. Then cut the stalks, with the ears still on, and arrange them into shocks—just like you see on Amish farms today or in those romantic farmy calendar pictures. To start a shock, I leave a few stalks uncut as a sort of stabilizing center, then lean the cut stalks around this center. After the shock is formed, tie it tightly toward the top for more stability. This tying also gives the shock a teepee-like form, which sheds rain. The ears of corn inside will continue to dry, and will be safe to store in rodent-free barrels by Christmas. Children love to "play Indians" in the teepee shocks, and their crawling in and out provides more air to the inside.

The ears can be husked out of the shock during the winter if you have no time before then. I like to leave a few shocks of sweet-corn stalks standing in the garden until spring, for birds (and garter snakes, I've learned) to use as shelters from the cold.

If fifty pounds or less of cornmeal is your goal, you can shell the corn by hand or with a hand-operated sheller, and store the kernels in a freezer where they will stay fresh and protected from bugs and rodents. I store the corn we use for meal on the cob, in open bushel-baskets in our food storage cellar. We've never had bug problems.

## Grinding and Eating

We grind our cornmeal on a hand-cranked Bell steel-cut gristmill, as we do our wheat, and sometimes oats and buckwheat. Stone-ground meal would possibly be better. (Aficionados argue this point endlessly.) Many kitchen mills are available. I suppose I would recommend an electric model, especially if you are older, because you will be inclined to use it more often than a hand-cranked one, and that probably is more important than conserving the little bit of power the electric model uses. Until recently, we have not presoaked the grain, but as we learn about fermenting grains, that's going to change. When presoaking corn, it is supposed to be extra nutritious if you add a little dolomitic limestone to the water—about one teaspoon per cup of corn flour, says Sally Fallon. If corn is the principle processed grain you eat, the addition of the lime is more important.

Even without soaking, cornmeal makes good hoecake and cornbread. We also use it in fermented batters (beer batter is my favorite), especially when frying our pond fish and the morel mushrooms we find in the woods.

Corn relish is another delicious way to enjoy fermented corn. No grinding necessary. The corn and other ingredients are pressed or pounded lightly to release their juices using the same principle as for making sauerkraut. Spices, condiments, and water are added, and the whole is left to stand at room temperature for a couple of days of fermentation. Then the jars are transferred to cold storage. Many vegetables can be fermented to add flavor, variety, and nutrition to them. While sauerkraut is probably the best known, most any vegetable (including peppers, carrots, and grape leaves) can be fermented similarly, without vinegar. Fermented foods of this nature keep a fairly long time, with less work and expense than freezing or canning.

Hominy is a corn food found more often in the South than in the North, for reasons unknown to me. Hominy is essentially corn kernels with the outer husks removed. Evidently, Native Americans invented hominy. They soaked the corn in water and wood ashes, and the lye from the ashes softened and removed the husks. My mother-in-law made hominy by soaking corn in lye water, too. In more modern times, hominy lovers soak the shelled corn (yellow or white field corn) overnight in baking soda (the old *Farm Journal* cookbook calls for two tablespoons of baking soda per quart of shelled corn and two quarts of water). In the morning, bring the mixture to a boil and cook for it three hours, or until the hulls loosen. Drain off the water, wash the corn in cold water, and rub off the husks. Bring the corn to a boil in two quarts of water again; drain, and repeat. Add salt to taste.

Mother-in-law fried the hominy in an iron skillet with bacon drippings and butter, or creamed it as you would creamed corn. (Delicious.) Cookbooks give many other recipes for making hominy dishes. My wife says that as a child, her family loved a very cheap meal of fried hominy, brown beans, and cooked kale seasoned with onions and vinegar. Hominy, she says, was used at their table much the way people today use rice or potatoes.

Wishing to waste nothing, the thrifty farm housewife makes jelly out of corncobs. Corncob jelly requires an ample amount of sugar or honey, which I imagine is the allure of this unusual food. But proponents insist that the jelly does have its own distinctive taste, sugar or no sugar.

Even corn husks are useful, for making surprisingly beautiful wreaths and other decorations. The inner soft white strips can be folded and arranged in hundreds of artful ways. Husk strips splashed with green, blue, and red markings (as the result of fungal activity) are especially desired. You can learn all about this art in craft books.

### Corn Whiskey

I can't resist pointing out that corn makes bourbon whiskey, and the reason I want to mention it is that whiskey could make a small garden farm into a profitable enterprise today. The ink was hardly dry on the Bill of Rights, guaranteeing us personal freedoms, when the government struck the first blow against small independent farmers by taxing their whiskey enterprises to death. The Whiskey Rebellion has never been given the importance it deserves in American history, which is a shame, because it shows so well how the combination of official greed and unrealistic morality breeds totalitarianism.

Today, the price of good bourbon is profanely high—$17 for a fifth (less than a quart) of Wild Turkey in Ohio. Better brands (in my opinion, such as Old Fitzgerald) aren't even available in most government-controlled liquor outlets in Ohio, which indicates that taxation is doubly inefficient in achieving even its own goals. Taxes ultimately represent almost half the price you pay for whiskey—that's the best estimate I can get after five calls to state officials. Our local liquor outlet manager didn't know. A Seagram's official didn't know. There are federal and state excise taxes, as well as state and local sales taxes that vary from place to place, so it appears no one person in the whole United States really does know the exact figure. And the government evidently doesn't want us to know.

"Good" people condone flagrant taxation of spirits because they insist that liquor is evil (even as they drink wine in religious ceremonies). As a result of our unrealistic attitudes, has drunkenness decreased? Of course not. It is the families of the drunks who suffer, as more and more of the family income goes into buying whiskey. Meanwhile the excise taxes support huge federal and state bureaucracies that eventually perpetrate idiocies such as blowing up a bunch of stupid and mostly harmless people in Waco, which in turn generates even more hideous idiocies such as blowing up Oklahoma City. Furthermore, the whiskey companies, who fear the legalization of "bootleg" liquor even more than the government does, cut the quality of their product to make a bigger profit. I have tasted really good moonshine, and I know the difference.

Have you any idea how profitable a corn patch could be if turned into good, smooth, $20-a-quart whiskey? One acre can produce two hundred bushels of corn. Every bushel could produce three gallons of bourbon. That's $240 per bushel, or $48,000 per acre. Left over would be maybe forty-five pounds of spent mash per bushel. This mash is an excellent animal feed, and in truth could be human food. What a dynamite porridge *that* would make.

My Kentucky father-in-law, now deceased, made good bourbon in

Depression days, and so could you. It wouldn't be that difficult if you didn't have to keep your operation hidden from the Alcohol, Tobacco, and Firearms gendarmes. Much of the bad moonshine that could blind you results from using methods to speed up the distillation process, to stay one step ahead of the revenuers. But my father-in-law did it right. He helped pay for his farm with bootleg liquor, risking jail at every turn. Nevertheless, he was one of the most virtuous people I've had the privilege of knowing. He enjoyed a drink of good bourbon every day. His daughter, my wife, taught me this healthful and pleasurable habit, and she is an even more virtuous person than her father. I've never seen either one of them even close to being intoxicated. (Maybe a little giggly.) Daddy-in-law lived healthfully to the age of eighty-seven. Smoking killed him, or he would have lived to be a hundred.

Whiskey would have been an excellent way to "save the family farm" and keep Appalachia economically vibrant, instead of turning it into a welfare sinkhole. Whiskey could save some suburban and exurban homes, too, for those who can't find good jobs and are subsisting on the crumbs that government and big business throw their way.

There are glimmers of enlightenment on the horizon. In some states, regulations have been relaxed for small wine makers and beer brewers. There are villages I know (New Riegel, Ohio, used to be the best example) where every home had a garden, and every garden a nice grape arbor, and every grape arbor produced a barrel of wine in the cellar.

Homebrewed beer is becoming popular—witness the evolution and revolution of microbreweries. I would not be surprised to see gardens of hops bloom again. Hops used to be grown in northern Ohio, and "wild" hop vines still mark the spots where it's been done. So why not corn and rye for whiskey? Shall we continue to follow the illogic of some Methodists I know: Wine is fine, but whiskey too risky?

## Backyard Wheat

Next to corn, wheat is the most widely grown grain in the United States. (Rice is the most common worldwide.) There are five principle classes of wheat: hard red winter and hard red spring, used for bread; soft red winter, used mostly for pastries; white wheat, used for breads as well as pastries; and durum wheat (also referred to as semolina), used mainly for pastas. Winter wheats are planted in the fall, go dormant over the winter, and then start growing again in the spring for summer harvest. Spring wheats are planted in the spring, in regions where winter wheats won't overwinter. Durum wheat is grown almost exclusively in North Dakota and surrounding areas. White wheats are grown mostly in New England. Hard red winter is grown west of the Mississippi, and soft red winter east of the Mississippi.

The properties of these wheats favor certain uses, which nevertheless are not mutually exclusive. The hard wheats have more protein, which means they generate more gluten during bread making. The more gluten, the stronger the dough. Durum wheat, at 12 to 15 percent protein, produces the most gluten, so it is strong enough to be stretched out in long ribbons, cut into strips, and hung up to dry on racks without breaking. Soft wheats work well in pastries, where gluten strength is not as critical, and may not even be desirable, as in flaky cakes.

Most baked goods are mixtures of various wheats combined to get just the right gluten content and consistency that the particular bread or pastry calls for. But at home, in small amounts, you needn't be as particular as master bakers. We use regular unbleached flour for pasta-making, and with the addition of eggs in the dough, think our pastas are almost as toothy as those made with semolina. Good bread-making cookbooks give all the fine points about flour and dough. I recommend also a relatively new magazine, *Fine Cooking* (Taunton Magazines, 63 South Main Street, Newtown, Connecticut 06470-9906), not only for grain cookery but for preparations of all backyard foods.

For years, I simply ground up whole wheat berries and sprinkled them raw on cooked oatmeal for my breakfast. Then I found that wheat could be "popped" just like corn, by putting it in a skillet with a little grease and roasting it. The wheat berries only expand a wee bit, unlike popcorn, yet a true popping expansion occurs. Then ground into whole meal, the wheat berries are more palatable, and I'm sure more easily digested. Soaking and drying them to make bulghur is better still, but roasting them is faster.

## *Planting and Cultivation*

To obtain seeds of grain for planting, the easiest route is via the nearest farm supply store or grain elevator, unless you know a farmer you can buy from directly. Wheat and other small grains sold specifically for seed are almost always treated with toxic pesticides not necessary for backyard production. Just buy plain *feed* grains. (You can feed any surplus to your animals.) Although you won't know which variety you are planting, it will almost always be a locally grown one, which is fine. However, if you want to grow a wheat from another region, for instance a bread wheat in a pastry wheat region, you can do so. The yield might not be what you expect, but then again it might be. Wheat is very cosmopolitan and adventuresome, suffering much less than other plants from provincialism. Health-food stores often carry grains for milling, and you can use these for seed, too.

When you plant a plot of wheat in your yard, just pretend you are seeding grass. That's what wheat is: a grass. In early autumn (or early spring, for spring wheat), lightly stir up some loose soil with the tiller. Broadcast the seed by scattering it with your hand, or by using one of those little broadcast seeders available from farm and seed supply centers. Broadcasting the wheat, you should try to get an average of one seed per square inch on the plot, or perhaps a little more. The proper measurement is about two bushels per acre, so if you figure that way, you will have to know the size of your plot.

After spreading the seed on top of the ground, rake or rotary-till very lightly to cover most of the seeds with a bit of dirt. If you can spread a little manure or compost over the plot after seeding, so much the better. But if the plot has been in a mulch bed for a number of years before, extra fertilizer will not be needed. In fact, without an intervening crop of corn between vegetables and wheat in your rotation, to "eat" some of that fertility, the soil might actually be too rich for small grains. With heavy fertilization, small grains often grow rank and fall over.

On the other hand, you should not experience any disease or insect problems. Wheat is easy to grow organically.

Once planted, the grain plot requires no more work until harvest, except to overseed a legume in the early spring if you wish to do so. It is especially important to sow this green manure crop if you intend to rotate your grain plot back to vegetables. Red clover works best for me, but alfalfa or ladino clover (or crimson clover in the South) work well, too. Broadcast the clover in April or March or even February (the traditional day here in northern Ohio is March 19, St. Joseph's Day). My father liked to broadcast clover seed when the field was still covered with snow, because then he could see where the tiny, dark-colored seeds fell, and thus could make sure he got a good covering. I like to overseed when the ground has thawed and then frozen again lightly, creasing the soil surface with little pits and pockmarks. The seed falls into these tiny fissures, and when the ground thaws again, the fissures flow together, covering the seeds with a light film of soil. But the seed will usually "catch" whenever you sow in spring, as long as rain provides moisture. The usual rate for sowing clover or alfalfa is eight pounds per acre, but when broadcasting rather than drilling, twelve pounds is better. On a small plot, the amount you need is obviously hardly more than a cupful. Consequently, it will be hard to spread evenly. Sow more than the plot calls for, and don't worry if the stand comes in too thick by commercial farm standards.

As the grain greens up in spring, the clover germinates too, but it will not be very noticeable until the wheat begins to die and the sun can penetrate better to the clover plants. As you cut your grain for harvesting, you cut the clover too, and any weeds trying to grow. Leave these cuttings for green manure, or feed them to your chickens. After the wheat harvest, the clover will grow back with great vitality, ahead of the weeds, and will keep the latter at bay.

### Harvesting and Threshing

The wheat is ready for harvest when the plants turn yellow-brown and die, and the grain heads begin to nod over. Rub a few heads of grain in your hand, blow away the chaff, and chew a few grains. They should be hard but crunchable. Further drying will take place after you cut the grain stalks and arrange them in shocks.

You can cut a small patch of wheat with a scythe or a cutter-bar mower. Rake the cut stalks into rough bundles (sheaves), and tie these with string or twine. Set the bundles into shocks, leaning two bundles against each other, then two more against the first two, and so on, building a shock of about ten bundles. Or you can rack the bundles up like cordwood under a roof.

Wheat harvest happens in July in the Midwest, earlier or later south to north. By August, if not sooner in a dry year, the grain in the bundles should be dry enough to thresh and store. We store threshed wheat in the freezer and in a second refrigerator to protect it from weevils, and so we don't worry about whether the grain is ideally dry (12 to 13 percent humidity) for storage.

In the absence of any reasonably priced small thresher on the market, you can lay the bundles out, one at a time, on a clean sheet, and whack the grain from the stalk heads with a plastic toy baseball bat. Then winnow out the chaff with a large window fan or a good breeze.

Another way to thresh is to stick the bundles, heads first, into a backyard shredder-grinder, to knock out the grain. This method will require a lot of winnowing, but that's a fairly easy job with a window fan. You can also make a threshing floor out of a panel of plywood or two, and run over the grain heads with lawnmower tires (rather than horses' hooves, as our forefathers did on their barn threshing floors). Alternatively, if you have a grass-catcher on your lawnmower, you can actually "mow" through the bundles. The straw, as chaff, and the grain end up in the bag where the grass clippings normally would, and you can dump this out and winnow away all but the grain.

The straw and chaff make good mulch for strawberries or bedding for the chicken coop. Michael Ellis, a researcher at Ohio State's research and development center at Wooster, Ohio, reports in *Fruit Grower* (May 1996), that "straw mulch provided a level of control of strawberry leather rot equal to any of the fungicides tested. In fact, fruits from the mulch plots looked much cleaner" (see chapter 4).

If you have more wheat than you need for making flour, you can feed extra bundles to chickens or quail or pigeons or rabbits, and let them thresh out the grains. The remaining straw becomes bedding. A handful of wheat or an ear of corn per day will keep a lawn-grazing chicken happy.

## Other Grains

### Barley, Rye, Spelt, and Triticale

These grains are all grown like wheat. Spelt is receiving greater interest these days because many people allergic to wheat can enjoy bread made from spelt. Triticale is a cross between wheat and rye. However, unless you are very fond of rye bread, are allergic to wheat, or want malt barley for beer, I don't really recommend growing any of these grains. You will get better results in a busy life by sticking with corn and wheat.

### Oats

Oats requires the same culture as wheat, but is usually (always, in the North) planted in the spring, with a legume planted at the same time. Thresh oats as you would wheat. The heart of the oat grain, or groat, is encased in a tight hull so when you grind whole oats, you may want to sift some of this hull out of the flour. For commercial oat foods, the grain is propelled at great force against an abrasive surface to separate the groat from the tight husk. But some people just roll or grind the whole oats roughly, and soak them overnight for porridge, never mind that outer hull. If the oats are roasted before soaking and cooking, I understand that the hull is of no consequence to the palate. I haven't done oats yet, so I can't say.

Cut with a sickle-bar mower or a scythe when the grain is nearly ripe, oats make excellent feed for rabbits, goats, and sheep. In fact, you could turn these animals into a stand, and they would harvest it themselves.

### Buckwheat

We have grown buckwheat for table use, and I suppose the fact that we haven't continued indicates that doing so is not particularly practical. Threshing the buckwheat is difficult, because the plant makes seed continuously rather than ripening to a single harvest. For table use, I strip the grains from the stalks periodically, enough for a couple of breakfasts of buckwheat cakes. Milled whole buckwheat contains a lot of hull, like oats, decreasing the palatability of the cakes somewhat. Passing the grain through a flour sifter removes some of the extraneous hull.

The advantage of buckwheat is that it can be planted late (up until about July 10 here), and still make a harvest. It makes a great second crop after vegetables, and if planted thickly, blots out late-germinating weeds. Buckwheat also is rich in cancer-preventing compounds.

Almost any edible seed can be grown as a backyard grain. Kamut, teff, and amaranth come to mind, of which the last is not technically a grain, since the plant is not a grass. But they all make interesting baked goods, as do millet, flax, and quinoa seeds. Someday an enlightened culture may make these and other "grains" part of everyday baked goods, but at the present, I don't want to spread the interest of new grain gardeners too thin. Stick with corn and wheat for now. There are enough varieties of these grains, and foods and drinks to make from them, to absorb your attention for a lifetime.

# CHAPTER 7

# GARDEN HUSBANDRY

The NIMBY (Not In My Back Yard) defense won't work for food. No matter how far away from us something bad is happening to what we eat, it eventually affects the most private part of our backyards—our bodies. If meat from animal factories becomes contaminated with drugs or hormones or harmful bacteria, you aren't free of the problem just because you have zoned your home away from the awful smell of anaerobic pit manure.

Fully half of the antibiotics used today are administered to animals. The conventional way that large numbers of hogs or chickens have been kept "healthy" in confinement buildings has been with more or less constant, subtherapeutic dosages of drugs. Science believes that this is a sure way to encourage bacterial resistance to antibiotics, and is urging more discipline in prescribing antibiotics to people. But for animals, it's mostly still business as usual, and bacterial resistance has now become more troubling in hog factories than it is in hospitals. The "solution" is always the same: to develop more powerful antibiotic medications. Medical science is now down to what researchers call the last line of defense: the class of antibiotics known as quinolones. So far, the quinolones have been reserved for human use only, but the hog industry is pressuring the FDA to relent and allow their use for animals, too.

If bacteria in an animal develops resistance to an antibiotic, can that resistance be transferred to a human eating the animal? Some scientists say yes; more say no. But whether or not there can be a direct, residual transfer, there is still danger. *Hogs Today* magazine (July 1995) quotes Stuart Levy at Tufts University Medical School: "Animal use produces multi-drug resistant bacteria that can reach humans via the food chain. If quinolones, the most important novel class of drugs available for humans, get into the hands of farmers and of the animal husbandry industry, they could be misused. If that happens and resistance becomes a problem, the concern is that it will spill over into people."

The other major concern is the use of growth hormones in the animal industry, or in human health, for that matter. Growth hormones exist naturally in humans and animals, but in very minute quantities. An excess appears to lead to abnormal growth. Some scientists believe that hormones in the food and waste streams, from animal growth regulators as well as from human medications, may be one of the causes of low sperm counts in men and of a general feminizing effect being observed in males of several species, including dwarfing of genitals in Florida alligators and Great Lakes fish that were exposed to estrogen compounds in wastewater. Hormonal medications, given to beef cattle to make them put on weight faster, is one source of estrogen compounds in the waste stream. So might be Bovine Growth Hormone (BGH or BST), injected in dairy cows to make them give more milk.

More alarmingly, some industrial chemicals contain what scientists call endocrine disruptors, which mimic the action of natural estrogens and disrupt normal growth, according to some recent findings. Although the meat industry has pooh-poohed this research, and many scientists doubt the validity of some of the studies making the connection, evidence is growing that there is a legitimate worry. At a 1991 meeting where the two sides debated the pros and cons, the following consensus statement was signed by twenty-one scientists: "We estimate with confidence that: Some of the developmental impairments reported in humans today are seen in adult offspring of parents exposed to synthetic hormone disruptors . . . released in the environment. The concentrations of the number of synthetic sex-hormone agonists and antagonists measured in the U.S. human population today are well within the range and dosages at which effects are seen in wildlife populations. . . . Unless the environmental load of synthetic hormone disruptors is abated and controlled, large scale dysfunction at the population level is possible." Since 1991, the evidence of some connection between "developmental impairments" and estrogen compounds appears to have grown stronger. In any event, sperm counts in men have been declining alarmingly, and the estrogen theory so far seems the most plausible explanation. (Read the detailed investigative report in *The New Yorker,* November 19, 1995.)

Talk about irony. Those advertisements you now see everywhere, of macho, brawny, meat-chewing male athletes with milk mustaches, may become only mockeries of the truth: cardboard fronts hiding low sperm counts and shrivelled genitals. Some women may think that's funny (can you blame them?), but endocrine disruptors have been linked to female breast cancer, too.

As if all that is not enough, here's a quote from my currently favorite cookbook, *Nourishing Traditions,* by Sally Fallon (Promotion Publishing, 1996): "Many [battery- or factory-raised chickens] . . . develop cancers and these [chickens] are not necessarily discarded. According to researcher Virginia Livingston Wheeler, these cancers can be transmitted to humans."

Whatever the scientific outcome of the preceding debates, I think that consumers worry too much about pesticide residue on their fruits and vegetables, but not enough about their commercial meat intake. Contrary gardeners should think about raising at least some of their own meat and other animal protein products, or buy meat from farms where antibiotics and hormones aren't used. Or become vegetarians.

Even if you take the vegetarian high road, you will benefit from making a place for husbandry in your garden. You can't keep husbandry out of the garden, in fact. Nature makes sure of that. The compost pile is full of microscopic animals. Your soil is full of earthworms and, alas, moles. Your trees are full of birds and squirrels. Your garden pool is (or should be) full of fish and frogs. Your bramble berries hide, alas again, a family of rabbits. Hopefully, your strawberry bed and vegetable plots have toads and garter snakes in residence. Bees and many other insects also are part of the husbandry of the garden. To add more wildlings and a few domesticated animals to this natural partnership of husbandry and horticulture is simply to recognize the reality of nature, and the holistic way in which the biological total is greater than the sum of its parts.

This partnership is, in any event, the only effective way to protest the assembly-line animal factories and to protect your diet from them. In the ruthless industrial economy beyond our gardens, there is no way to stop the trend toward megaconsolidation of everything. The madness will have to collapse of its own accord. A friend, a former employee of AT&T and now a farmer, tells me that the doctrine preached to him while he worked there was known as the Rule of Three. "We were told that by the year 2010, each area of economic activity would be controlled by three corporations," he says. I wonder, after AT&T downsized thousands of people out of work recently, if it still believes that it is one of those chosen corporations. Looks to me that by 2010 we will be down to the Rule of One, and that One will be the State.

But even if you don't care to get political about food and economic policy, or about holistic gardening, I would still urge you to think of husbandry as well as horticulture in your backyard, simply because it's fun.

## Chickens at Least

The Republican presidential campaign slogan in 1932 was "a chicken in every pot." A decade ago, this would have sounded quaint indeed, but as the financial situation leans more and more precariously toward those out-of-work days of the 1930s, the chicken-in-every-pot philosophy can be heard faintly behind the rhetoric of today's presidential campaign buffooneries. Interestingly, the slogan originated about 1600, when Henri IV of France was supposed to have said (probably with as much hypocrisy as our presidents talk today), "I want no peasant in my realm so poor that he will not have a chicken in his pot every Sunday." Henri's hope was repeated in the middle 1800s by Alexander Smith, a poet and essayist who wrote pompously, "Just consider what a world this would be if ruled by the best thoughts of men of letters. Ignorance would die at once, war would cease, taxation would be lightened, [and] not only every Frenchman but every man in the world, would have his hen in the pot."

Obviously, the chicken has been a part of human civilization for a long time and with it the conviction that there is no good reason for anyone going meat-hungry—no thanks to kings and poets, either. It is no wonder the Greek augurs studied the entrails of chickens to try to fathom the future. Chickens were important to the well-being of human society. That is why there are so many breeds, nearly a hundred still available today from mail-order sources such as Murray McMurray Hatchery (Webster City, Iowa 50595-0458). In fact, the widespread disappearance of the chicken from backyards has only been a momentary blip on the screen of human history—scarcely fifty years out of untold centuries, and then only in the so-called developed countries.

For those Americans with 1940s village life still vivid in their memories, the return of the little red hen should be as natural as a sunrise. My grandmother, in those days, kept quite a flock of hens at the end of her garden, right smack in the middle of town, and her whole property scarcely measured a quarter-acre. She made Easter eggs dyed a deep mahogany for all her numerous grandchildren. Although we knew she used onion skins for coloring, none of us have ever been able to duplicate that tint.

When I was very young and we were living in a walk-up over the bank, prior to moving out to the farm, my parents kept a cow in a barn right at the edge of town. Going to that barn for the milking must have been an exciting event for me, because in the first clear memory of my life, I am sitting in a pile of straw in that barn while Dad milks the cow and Mom forks hay into the manger. I remember that they were laughing.

No kind of garden husbandry is easier than keeping four to eight hens, which will provide enough eggs for a family except during molting from late November till early January. If you get four chicks every spring, they will begin to lay at about the time the four older hens molt, so you will never quite run out of eggs. When the young hens start laying, you can make chicken soup out of the old ones. You do not need a rooster unless you want to hatch the eggs. (A rooster is not desirable in urban backyards, because its crowing in the morning will generate unhappy neighbors and someone will want to enforce or introduce silly zoning regulations against chickens.)

You can let a few hens roam your yard or fenced-in portions of it. If they try to fly over the fence, clip their wings. Chickens will go back to their roosts as nightfall approaches. You can give them the run of the garden, where they will help the toads, salamanders, and garter snakes eat bugs and slugs. Maybe you should keep the chickens away when strawberries and tomatoes are in season, but four hens won't do much damage the rest of the time.

### The Chicken Coop

A chicken coop need be only a humble affair, but should provide at least ten square feet per chicken, which is more than ten times the commercial norm. With that much room and a deep-litter floor (details ahead) you will have no smelly manure problem. A four- to eight-hen flock will do fine in an 8- by 10-foot shed. Old Mr. Harrison, the neighbor who taught me so much about backyard food production when we lived in the Philadelphia suburbs, kept eight hens in a pen of those dimensions. But his coop was only three feet high, supported by posts three feet above the ground, so he could reach into it easily from doors on either end. He did not let his hens out. Along with a little grain, and table and garden scraps, he tossed into the coop what he called a sod—a spadeful of turf—every other day. He took out the old pecked and worn sod and used it to replace the divot in the lawn left by the new one. Since trace amounts of natural antibiotics occur naturally in good soil, I presume his chickens derived some from the sods, along with minerals and vitamins. The floor of his pen was wire so the manure dropped through and could be speedily collected and applied to garden or compost heap. There were roost poles for the hens to perch on so they didn't get sore feet from the wire.

We kept a dozen chickens in that suburban setting, in a coop measuring nine by eighteen feet. We bedded the dirt floor with sawdust and straw, adding new bedding every week or so until the litter was a foot deep. The deep litter would accept all the manure with no odors. We had no fenced runs but often let the chickens out two hours before sunset. Had we left them to run about all day at their leisure, they would have found a way to scratch every square inch of ground we owned, and speckle all horizontal planes, even lawn furniture and car roofs, with their droppings. In two hours, thrice a week, they did not have enough time to get mischievous or to find our neighbors' flower gardens. If, on rare occasion, they got through our "multideplora rose" hedge, the neighbors did not foment too much, because either they raised chickens themselves or ate our eggs. In my observations, neighbors get into problems over animals because someone always tries to overdo—raise more chickens or cats or whatever than they have room, time, or the neighborhood's tolerance for. So we get ordinances against chickens. (But never cats. Cats are to Americans what white cows are to India.)

There are many different ways to handle a few chickens. Only certain details are essential, such as the deep-litter method of bedding the floor of the chicken pen, though even this is not necessary in setups like Mr. Harrison's. Straw, wood shavings, sawdust, peat moss, well-dried lawn grass, shredded paper, or dry leaves—almost anything that will absorb moisture makes adequate bedding.

Let the bedding build up; keep adding more on top. The chickens scratch in the bedding continually, making the finest compost of it imaginable. We clean out the coop only once a year. Actually, I don't really clean it out, but just keep removing compost as I need it, and during winter add sawdust and straw. In the 1950s, quite to everyone's surprise, researchers found that chickens stayed healthier on deep-litter beds than in coops cleaned out monthly. Microorganisms in the litter produce vitamin B-12, for one thing, and vitamin K, for another. This compost makes the best material for your potting mixes.

Another must, where hens and growing chicks are raised in the same flock, is a coop with two rooms. If kept together, the hens will torment the growing chicks, and perhaps even kill them. If the separation between the two rooms is a wire fence only, the two flocks will get more accustomed to each other than if the partition is solid wood. As the chicks grow to pullet size, the two groups can be allowed to gradually come together, usually by introducing them to each other outdoors. Each room in the coop should have its own exit to the outside, and a connecting door between them.

A properly designed coop, especially in the North, should have lots of window space on the south side, facing the sun. The windows should open for ventilation by leaning them inwards a little at the top. They don't even have to be hinged, but need a braced bracket built out from the wall at the top of the window, or a chain attached to the wall and the window top, to keep the window from falling all the way into the building. The hens are unlikely to figure out that they could fly up and escape through such an opening, and rain can't normally come in that way. (My fingers are crossed as I write this because in husbandry, anything that can happen will happen at least once.) Other ventilation should be provided under the roofline all around the top of the walls, screened over so sparrows, rats, and other vermin can't get in. The coop by all means should stand under a shade tree, as midsummer heat waves can have critical effects in a small coop. Plant deciduous trees on the south side of the coop right away if you don't have any to take advantage of. This is an excellent place for peach trees, incidentally, because the hens will scratch the soil bare around them (peach trees don't do as well surrounded by sod) and will eat peach-tree-borer eggs and larvae that hatch in the soil at the base of the trees.

If you feel you need to have a plan for building, study any of the old chicken coops you can see on farmsteads as you drive through the countryside. If you still feel hesitant, read *Rural New England* magazine, whose editor Robert Kaldenbach is the world's Most Practical Backyard Chicken Expert, in my opinion. The January 1996 issue is an excellent one to start with. "The housing is easy to build, and to destroy when you come to hate the foul fowl," says Kaldenbach in his typical droll humor.

The simplest of all coops is Andy Lee's *Chicken Tractor* (see his book with the same name, published by Good Earth Publishing and available from Chelsea Green). The Chicken Tractor is a tongue-in-cheek name for his simple, moveable, bottomless chicken pens. Various sizes and designs are possible. The idea is to rotate the pens, with their chicken occupants, from one garden bed or plot to another when the beds are not growing crops. The chickens eat weed seeds, grass, garden waste, or whatever is present, along with feed given them if necessary. They cultivate and bare the soil for planting with their incessant scratching for worms, and they fertilize the bed with their droppings. In this system, the chickens can be introduced in the spring, and butchered or sold in the fall, dispensing with the need for a permanent, overwintering coop. (Even if you don't want to raise chickens in a Chicken Tractor, this book is excellent from the standpoint of discussing how fowl husbandry fits into gardening.)

I am often amazed at how books about chickens needlessly complicate and worry the subject. All those pages of caveats are necessary for the grower who wants to make a profit from the enterprise, where that profit requires crowding the chickens together unnaturally, or pushing them to production heights that nature never intended. But if you grow a few chickens in lots of space, and in a way that mimics nature closely, you will not need to even know about all those diseases that can sicken and kill chickens. (Did you ever see a sick woodpecker?) You don't have to feed your flock commercial, milled, or pelleted feed either, except maybe to get the chicks started off. If I raised only four chicks every year, I'd start them on oatmeal and milk. But this gets a little expensive for thirty chicks. Our hens get only whole corn and wheat to supplement their natural grazing diet, plus our table scraps.

Nor do you need to invest in brooder heaters. Wait till warm weather to get chicks, and keep them in the garage under a 60-watt bulb for a few days before transferral to the coop.

If you do not provide your hens with a nest box or two, they will find a nook and make their own nests—all over the floor. A 5-gallon bucket, laid on its side and nailed to a shelf or brace on the wall in any rudimentary manner, makes a good nest. The bucket, open at only one end, remains relatively dark inside. The hen likes that, and the darkness discourages her from eating eggs. An old nail keg will also do the job. Any wooden box about a foot and a half long and a foot wide, laid on its side, works okay. Put a bit of a lip at the lower front of the box, so the hens don't drag eggs and nesting materials out. If using a bucket, install it with the open end a bit higher than the back end. Keep clean dry straw, shavings, hay, excelsior, or some such in the nest.

Don't think of your backyard chickens as money makers, but as quality food for which there is no price. You don't have to follow some of the complicated practices of commercial flocks. You don't have to debeak your chickens. You don't have to leave a light on at night to encourage the hens to keep eating and lay more eggs. And you don't have to have a floor in the coop. A dirt floor is best: a concrete or wood floor provides a handy place underneath for rats and mice. A footer (a masonry foundation two feet deep) is nice, in that it will prevent rats and raccoons from digging under the walls and getting in. But in thirty years with coops of only pole construction, and no foundation and no floor, only a couple of times have wild animals attempted to dig under the wall of our coop, and only once has any harm come from those attempts. (For the bottom siding boards on our walls, the ones half-buried in the soil, we used pressure-treated 2 x 6s.) Be sure to close in with wire mesh all ventilation openings under the eaves; otherwise, coons will scale the wall and get in through the vent openings. Remember also to secure all doors and windows at night. A coon is perfectly capable of killing all the hens in the coop in one raid, out of sheer ecstasy.

You should make sure to site your coop so it doesn't sit in a low spot in the landscape. You don't want a pool of water in there after a downpour. Raise the floor area above the surrounding landscape with the soil dug for the poles, plus other soil and gravel if necessary. If you have several acres of meadow, a good idea is to build a moveable chicken coop—a large Chicken Tractor—and drag it on a regular schedule from one place to another around the field. Joel Salatin, a now-famous contrary farmer, has commercialized this method of raising chickens (see his book *Pastured Poultry Profits: Net $25,000 in Six Months on Twenty Acres,* published by Polyface and available from Chelsea Green). Part of that net comes from using your own labor to butcher the chickens, which on a commercial level represents lots of work.

Where most backyard hen-raisers make a mistake, in my opinion, is following the commercial coop design that calls for a manure-catching floor under the roosts. This arrangement is necessary when hens are crowded, but it results in a buildup of pure manure on the catching boards—a vile-smelling mess. In roomy, deep-litter coops, the chicken roost need be only 2 x 4s long enough to accommodate all the hens, stretched over a corner of the coop about two feet above the floor. You *want* the droppings to fall into the bedding in a deep-litter system. The chickens then scratch it into the bedding—no muss, no fuss.

### Feeding Your Brood

You can use about any container for a feeder: metal, plastic, or wood. For a few hens, a waterer can be made by cutting off the bottom half of any plastic gallon receptacle with a pocketknife. When water freezes in these containers in winter, I bang them on something solid to crack the ice out of them. Eventually, the plastic cracks, but such containers are plentiful. With this method of watering, I don't have to buy an expensive heating device or a heated waterer. Since I put fresh water in the container both morning and night, the hens never stay long with only ice to try to sip. When we go on summer trips overnight or for a couple of days, I will use a regular purchased chicken-waterer or two, or place several buckets of water in the coop—plenty enough to last until we return. Some growers hang their waterers and feed troughs from the ceiling, just high enough to allow the chickens to reach them. This arrangement prevents the chickens from upsetting the waterers or scratching bedding into feeders. Sometimes I don't even use troughs, but just scatter the whole grain on the floor to encourage the hens to scratch in the litter.

After you have fed your hens for a few days, you will know how much they can clean up in an hour or so. You don't want to leave excess grain in the troughs for long periods of time, because that could draw rats or mice or English sparrows. By the same token, get a metal or tough plastic barrel or similar rat-proof container to store your grain in.

If you keep four hens part of the year, and eight the rest of the year, as I've been using for an example, they will eat about six bushels of corn or wheat annually. Feeding table scraps and letting the hens graze part-time, or bringing fresh grass clippings, good clover hay, earthworms, and garden waste to them when penned, can cut the grain requirement by half or more. In addition, you will want to feed your hens some oyster shells, available from the farm supply store; also feed them all their own egg shells for extra calcium. Tiny bits of stone (grit) help chickens digest their food, and they will get what they need roaming their outdoor run or the lawn and garden. If not, throw a little sand or fine gravel in the coop.

### Chickens to Eat

It's no problem to raise some broilers for meat, in addition to your laying hens. Since it takes only two to three months to fatten a broiler, depending on breed, space requirements for them are not great. We raise thirty broilers a year, along with the dozen or so laying hens in our coop of two hundred square feet. By the time the broilers are big enough to crowd the coop, they're gone.

I hate to butcher chickens, but I can handle thirty or so a year. Carol and I will do four or five a morning for the several mornings it takes. We can kill, scald, pick, and clean that many hens in about an hour, but Carol spends another hour cleaning up the carcasses while they cool in clean, cold water. When all the body heat is out of them, into the freezer they go, except for the ones we eat fresh.

There is usually someone in every rural neighborhood who custom-butchers chickens. (In my region, the Amish offer this service.) Learning to do it yourself requires watching someone else first, or you can follow one of these good manuals on home-butchering: *Butchering, Processing and Preservation of Meat* by Frank G. Ashbrook (Van Nostrand Reinhold, 1955); and *Home Butchering and Meat Preservation* by Geeta Dardick (TAB Books, 1986). Both books provide illustrations to help you along.

With most of this country's poultry being processed mechanically on assembly lines, I am amazed that salmonella outbreaks are as rare as they are—especially since, in my experience, the chances of intestinal wastes contacting the meat are greater when butchering chickens than with any other commonly eaten meat. My hat's off to the industry, but I don't want to know what really goes on in those poultry factories. When you cook meat, make sure you cook it long and hot enough to kill salmonella.

Asking what kind of chickens you should raise is like asking what kind of car you should drive. Go with whatever strikes your fancy. My fancy favors the traditional breeds that are considered dual-purpose hens:

heavier birds that are fairly good egg-layers, too. Rhode Island Red and Plymouth Rock are the two most popular such breeds. But if you find that you enjoy raising chickens, consider branching out. Many weird and wonderful breeds are available. Maybe even start exhibiting your less common varieties at the local fair. If you have the only White Crest Black Polish chicken entered, you are almost bound to win a ribbon. You might even make some money, in spite of yourself, if you decide to raise rare breeds such as Ancona, Black Minorca, Delaware, Dominique, Black Jersey Giant, Brown Leghorn, and White Wyandot. You can find out more from the American Livestock Breeds Conservancy (Box 477, Pittsboro, North Carolina 27312).

For broilers, we have been raising the White Mountain breed, but I'm not saying that's the best choice. I don't know if there ever is such a thing as the best. These broilers have been so genetically manipulated for fast growth that their legs sometimes give out as the birds get heavy, and they plop around like frogs. Or their toes curl up like club feet. They don't forage well, but will squat at the trough and stuff themselves with commercial feed, if you let them, until they can barely walk. They fatten to four pounds in eight weeks, and their meat is tender and nicely moist if prepared properly. However, connoisseurs claim that the meat is not as tasty as that from slower-growing chickens, and this may be true. On the diet that we feed our broilers, which forces them to forage for some of their food, the White Mountains produce a meat that tastes great when Carol Southern-fries it in her inimitable way. New fast-fattening breeds that supposedly don't get foot and leg problems are now available, although growers have complaints about them, too. They don't grow fast enough.

Tough old hens and roosters are good for making soup, but stewing the meat in wine is the traditional way to use them. That's how *coq au vin* started—as a way to get rid of what would otherwise be low-quality meat, not as the gourmet delight that it has become. You can cook the hell out of an old rooster in a wine stew, and it only gets better-tasting.

Parker Bosley, the famous chef of Parker's Restaurant in Cleveland, and a friend of mine, makes *coq au vin* using this recipe:

8 leg and thigh pieces from old hens
½ cup vegetable oil
8 thick slices bacon, cut in 1-inch pieces
½ cup flour for dusting the meat
20 small onions or chunks of large onions
4 tablespoons butter
1 pound mushrooms
2 tablespoons flour
1 cup Madeira wine
3 to 4 cups chicken stock and/or water
2 cups red wine
2 tablespoons dried thyme
1 bay leaf
salt and pepper

Heat the oil in a heavy-bottomed sauté pan. Add the bacon. Keep the heat low and slowly render out the bacon fat. Remove the bacon and set aside; save renderings for the pan. Season the chicken pieces with salt and pepper, and flour them well. Brown the chicken slowly over medium heat, in the bacon-flavored oil. To avoid crowding, cook the chicken in batches. As the pieces brown, remove them to an ovenproof baking dish. While the chicken browns, peel the onions. Be careful not to remove all the root end, to prevent the onions from coming apart. Finish browning the chicken and pour off the oil. Add 3 tablespoons of the butter to the pan; add the onions. Keeping the heat low, toss the onions continuously. When the onions are slightly colored, remove them to the baking dish with the chicken. Sauté the mushrooms in the pan, using a little more butter if necessary, for two to three minutes; then add them to the baking dish, along with the cooked bacon.

In the sauté pan, melt the remaining butter and brown the flour. Keep the heat low to avoid burning. When the flour has browned, add the Madeira and stir with a wire whisk; continue whisking and cooking for 5 minutes. Add the chicken stock and the red wine to the pan. Pour this sauce into the baking dish. Last, add the thyme and bay leaf, and season with salt and pepper. Cover and put the baking dish into a preheated 250-degree Fahrenheit oven. Cook for about 90 minutes, or until the chicken is nearly falling from the bone. The toughness of the chicken will determine the actual cooking time.

Undercooking the chicken and refrigerating it for a day, to be reheated for dinner, will help develop the flavors. Remove the baking dish from refrigerator 2 hours before serving. Let the dish come to room temperature. To reheat, put the dish in the oven; turn the temperature up to 250 degrees Fahrenheit. After 20 minutes, raise the temperature to 350 degrees. Make sure the dish is very hot and completely cooked before serving. Serve with rice or boiled potatoes.

Parker, who was born and raised on a farm in Ohio, buys chicken for his restaurant from small, mostly local, growers. Chefs like him are increasing in number, and may give you an idea of how to turn backyard chicken farming into a little business. To go with *coq au vin* and other dishes, Parker also purchases mushrooms from local specialty farmers, and wines from Ohio vineyards. His purpose is always to encourage local economies. "When I lived in southern France, the most interesting restaurants relied on locally grown food and advertised it as such," he says. "Often you could go down the road a mile and find where the food you ate came from." He deplores factory-farm chicken. "But rather than stew in the politics and policies of the poultry industry, better give your attention to the stew pot with the chicken and the wine. While the chicken is simmering, sit down at the kitchen table and write a letter to the [U.S.] Department of Agriculture and to the department of poultry science at your state university. Tell them that the market they control is not serving you."

## Pigeons

In Amishland in Ohio (mainly Holmes County), there are weekly auctions where a fantastic variety of food goods is offered for sale. The best, in my opinion, is the Mt. Hope auction, but there are others. Among the wide assortment of fowl are common pigeons. The Amish farm boys, never ones to miss an opportunity, catch the pigeons in their barns where the birds live in a semi-wild state, feasting on grain growing in the fields or dropped inadvertently in the barnyard. The boys catch the birds with long-handled fishing nets, and sell them for about $1.50 each. Most pigeons are purchased by shooting clubs for live bird-shooting, but some are bought for eating. An Amish friend of mine chuckles about this trade: "Yes, the boys catch the pigeons and sell them at auction, but the population of pigeons in our barns does not diminish. My theory is that when the birds are let loose on shooting reserves, the hunters miss most of the time, and the pigeons of course fly right back home. I have a hunch the boys have sold some of those pigeons half a dozen times."

These are the same common pigeons that foul public buildings. Cities and towns must then spend a fortune to clean up the mess. Lately in the news, I note that in some areas, people have finally wised up and started catching and eating the pigeons, but this has caused an outrage among the spoiled, fastidious, overcivilized upper crust. I know people who approve of timber companies that endanger rare species of animals by overharvesting wood but who protest loudly over feeding poor people overpopulated pest animals.

The ability of pigeons to prosper among humans should not be lost on contrary gardeners. That ability certainly was used to advantage in days gone by. In the Middle Ages, pigeons were almost free food as they flew from their dovecotes to forage for grain, weed seeds, and insects in countryside and village. In fact, the poorer peasants were not allowed to keep pigeons, and hated the birds, or rather, the rich lords and ladies who kept them. By the hundreds, the pigeons flew from the round, silo-like dovecotes (the first giant agribusiness animal factories), raiding the peasants' little grain plots and vying with the poor for the stray grain they were allowed to glean from the lordly manors after harvest.

Until recently, and still among traditional farm people such as the Amish, barns were built with dovecotes in them. Such a dovecote might mean only cutting a hole in the barn wall, large enough for pigeons to enter high up under the eaves, and providing some kind of little platform inside for them to nest and strut upon. You don't actually have to provide a place for pigeons to roost and nest if the barn has horizontal beams that they can use high up on the walls. As a child, I often sat quietly in our haymow, listening to that wonderfully peaceful sound of cooing pigeons. Mother was constantly after us to climb up to the pigeon nests and bring her a pair of squabs for pigeon pie. We never did, I guess because we had so many chickens to eat. As the old barns and old farming ways declined, the pigeons did just what the farmers did: They went to the city.

Cookbook author and nutritionist Sally Fallon tells me that in South America, pigeons are used to make broth:

> Just follow the recipe in my book for chicken broth. To prepare, remove the guts and feathers and boil the whole bird, including the head, with some garden vegetables for about 24 hours. But if you have a cat, give him the head raw—he will go crazy over this. Always add a little vinegar to bring out the calcium. Strain, let congeal and remove the fat. Separate the bones and skin from the pigeon meat and give them to your dog—they'll be soft enough. You can also fill a ring mould with the pigeon meat, plus some vegetables grated or cut up, and pour in the broth, perhaps with a little extra gelatin added, and also some salt. Refrigerate, and voila! *Pigeon en Gelee.*

Pigeon and squab producers today rely more on domestic pigeon breeds including Silver Kings, White Kings, Blue Kings, Carneaux, Mondains, Giant American Crests, Giant Homers, Hungarians, Maltese, Florentines, and more modern crosses. The wild pigeons of town and country are a mongrel breed of varied colors—"rock doves" is a somewhat more accurate label for them—not as large or broad breasted. But for home use, they make meat as good as any. I've read stories about urbanites who started feeding "wild" pigeons in city backyards, and finally had to quit because hundreds flocked to their feeding stations. Other city dwellers, with souls of farmers, keep pigeons in wire and wood-frame hutches on the roofs of tenement houses, along with little raised-bed, containerized roof gardens. This is a most elemental and genuine example of combining horticulture and husbandry in contrary gardening, bested only by the Vietnamese, who when first arriving in American cities as immigrants, killed stray cats and dogs for food. The pampered tribes of overweight and beef-flushed Americans howled in protest, even when presented with the fact that city officials and humane societies must spend millions of dollars annually killing and incinerating overpopulations of strays.

### Raising Pigeons

Raising domestic pigeons is much like raising chickens. The advantage pigeons have, unless you are raising rollers (so-called from their strange acrobatics in flight) or homing or squab-producing pigeons as a business or hobby, is that you can let them fly free through the neighborhood, be it urban or rural, as wild pigeons do, and feed themselves. Sort of like keeping bees. You don't have to learn how to raise them, just accommodate them. I know it works because friends of ours kept a few domestic pigeons that way, not for food but just for fun. The birds might be gone all day, foraging through their suburban/country neighborhood, but would come back at dusk. Kept with chickens, the pigeons were content to stay home and eat chicken feed some of the time. Making salt available at all times is helpful in keeping wildish pigeons coming back home, but if they are homers to begin with, you can't stop them from returning to the coop.

Homing pigeons are a fascinating study. The homing instinct in these birds is uncanny. In Cornell University experiments, homers dropped off six hundred miles away flew back in less than ten hours. Even when nearly blinded with frosted contact lenses that blurred all visual landmarks, the birds could still return to within a few feet of their loft from as far away as one hundred miles. The record homing flight, set by a Signal Corps pigeon during World War II, is twenty-three hundred miles. And science can't explain how the birds do it.

Kept in captivity, pigeons need an airy exterior flyway of wire mesh, framed with wood, maybe ten feet high minimum and three hundred feet square, so they can fly around a little. Any building loft, darkened somewhat and provided with nest boxes and nesting material (such as straw), will work fine in connection with the outside flyway. A chicken coop with a second story under the gables, equipped with nests and strutting space, serves both birds: chickens downstairs and pigeons upstairs. As with chickens, about any old box or bucket will do for a nest. Homing pigeons need two nests per pair, as very productive ones may well begin hatching one set of eggs while squabs still occupy the first nest. This is why pigeons tend to overpopulate and paint the town (or farm machinery in the country) white and grey. The parents feed the young themselves, which is another reason they should be favored by contrary gardeners: Don't do yourself what nature will do for you.

You can buy pigeons of all kinds from places such as Stromberg's Chicks and Pets (P.O. Box 717, Fort Dodge, Iowa 50501), and once you see their catalogs, you will realize the great amount of information available about pigeons and squab production, and the array of equipment available to help you.

### Eating Pigeons

Pigeon pie, made like we make chicken pot pie (the top crust requires three sticks of butter), is a heavenly dish. Under such a crust, old skunk meat would taste good.

## Coturnix Quail

In 1975, when I was visiting the home of Bob Rodale of Rodale Press fame, I heard an oddly familiar cheep, cheep. I stopped in mid-sentence and stared at my host. "If I weren't sitting in your house, Bob, I'd swear I just heard a quail chick," I said, mystified. I knew what a quail chick sounded like because just that spring as I'd walked my hay field, a quail had flushed ahead of me and flown awkwardly, as if its wing was broken. As I'd stood there, puzzled, the clover around me began to pulsate with a thousand high, thin cheep-cheeps. To my astonishment I was surrounded by quail chicks so tiny that two of them could nestle in the palm of my hand. They could not have hatched more than twenty-four hours earlier. Old mother was feigning injury to lure me away.

Now as I stared at Bob and the cheeps broke into a similar chorus, he smiled like a little boy with a frog croaking in his pocket. "You are quite right," he said. "I'm raising some in the house. This appears to be, so far, about the simplest possible way to have your own fresh eggs."

And so it proved to be. Several pairs of coturnix quail, which are somewhat bigger than the American bobwhite and lay larger eggs, will adapt as easily as parakeets to living in a box or smallish wire cage in an airy, sunlit room, and keeping their pen clean of manure is not much more difficult than keeping a parakeet pen clean. Quail eggs taste just like chicken eggs, boiled, fried, or scrambled. Of course the eggs are only about as big as those a bantam hen lays, so you might want three or four for breakfast. Bob said that he had learned that quail eggs, by weight, had less cholesterol in them than hen eggs, and research at his experimental farm indicated that quail eggs were a little cheaper to raise by weight. Quail produce about a pound of eggs for every two pounds of feed. An average-sized hen requires over three pounds of feed to produce a pound of eggs.

A quail hen begins laying in about sixty days from hatching, a hundred days sooner than chickens, which accounts for most of the lower cost. Quails will lay an egg a day for about year. If four hens will keep you in eggs for a year, twelve quail will too. If you remove the eggs daily, the quail will keep on laying as long as they have good food and water in front of them. (You can't raise quail free-range of course; they would just fly off.) Those with experience say you will have better luck hatching eggs if you use an incubator. To start, you will be better off buying two pairs of quail, I think, rather than buying eggs to incubate them, but some quail raisers disagree. Again, I refer you to Stromberg's or McMurray's.

Coturnix quail will do better in winter inside the house than in an outdoor coop, but for about a dozen, a little pen in the backyard with a screened run connected to it will be fine. The chicks are so tiny that they can escape almost any enclosure, so until they get a little size to them, keep them in their coop or cage. The experts advise giving the birds a square foot per adult bird in a relaxed backyard, noncommercial operation, but I would double or triple that at least. Feed quail just as I have described for chickens, but because of their smaller size, milled grain would be better than whole grain, especially in the case of corn. Garden greens are fine, and table scraps too, just as for chickens. Quail love insects and a covey of wild bobwhites is a treasure every gardener should wish for.

In captivity coturnix quail grow to be large enough to eat in six weeks. Eat the cocks first, and let the hens keep laying. If you intend to hatch your own eggs, you will need to keep one cock for every two hens.

Ducks and geese and other fowl are also good candidates for garden husbandry, but all of these birds have some characteristics that makes them questionable for backyard production in a typical urban, suburban, or exurban setting. But if you're interested, go ahead. I'd love to be proved wrong.

## Rabbits

Wandering through Knott County, Kentucky, in 1974, I found a place that didn't belong to the United States that most of us know. I have long ago lost track of the family I found there, so I won't use their names. So unusual were they that I would be tempted to wonder whether I had only dreamed it all were it not for my yellowed field notes from those days. The thirtysomething sophisticated woman from the city was nursing a baby who had been born in this mountain fastness with only her husband in attendance. The other six children were playing beside a hillside spring as happy as puppies. They were more articulate than most children today, although I'm sure they had not seen the inside of a classroom for some time, if ever. They showed me a hummingbird nest hardly bigger than a thimble, and pawpaw trees laden with bananalike fruit in the goat pasture. When a brief rain shower scudded by, the goats all piled into the privy for protection.

The family called their place Homespun Rabbit Farm. They were making a shaky living spinning and weaving the fur from their Angora rabbits. The wool was worth $3 an ounce then, spun and dyed with mullein, chestnut bark, coreopsis, jewelweed, broom sedge, goldenrod, sumac, elderberries, ragweed, pokeberry, or walnut. A big iron kettle over a fire in the yard bubbled away with a soup of broomsedge, in which white Angora yarn was turning to a golden glow. "I can spin an ounce and a half an hour," the wife said. "A finished nightgown I sell for $60 and an afghan for $130." Her husband smiled goodhumoredly. "We make about 50¢ an hour, all told," he said.

Angora rabbit wool has an advantage over many other woven animal-hair fabrics. When wet, it doesn't smell as does wool, or worse, dog hair. It can be clipped but is usually plucked to get the longest hairs possible. When the hairs are used long, the fabric won't shed, the woman told me. Plucking doesn't seem to bother the rabbits—they pull out their own hair for nest lining. "Angora rabbits are the perfect livestock to go with a back-yard garden farm," said the husband. "They are easy and cheap to house and feed, the manure is super rich for the garden, and whether you are interested in the fabric or not, the meat is excellent tablefare."

Whether they succeeded in their unusual venture and eventually moved on to the farm they hoped to own I don't know. Looking back now, I believe their enterprise would have been more sustainable if they had approached it with the contrary gardener's goal of making a little supplementary income, rather than making a living from it. But at that time, they were successful in a much higher sense: their purpose was to raise their children outside the stressful, strident, strangulating environment of conventional schooling.

In most circumstances, raising rabbits seems to be one of those chores parents think their children should do for awhile to "gain experience." I don't know what experience they gain in a situation like this. Artificiality I guess. Generally, children without enthusiastic leadership and companionship from parents lose interest in their rabbit project when it becomes obvious that there's not any money in it unless they make a full time job of it, which at that age they can't do. Then Daddy or Mom sells the rabbit cages to another set of parents afflicted with the same romantic notion. I don't think this is the way to do it. It is the adult who should either raise rabbits or not, and let the children join as the spirit moves them. Then they will come back to gardening and husbandry when they are adults.

My theory is that rabbit projects don't last long because of those damnable cages. I don't know exactly how the idea of raising rabbits in cages became so universal as to be the only method now considered, but I suppose it started for lack of space. Among poorer people in countries such as Italy, for whom rabbit meat has always been a staple food, rabbits are crowded into cages ranked in tiers up off the ground, primarily because of lack of suitable land area.

Cages are a poor way to raise rabbits if you only want to keep a few. In cages, manure is harder to manage and stinks worse for lack of bedding to soak it up (although you can solve this problem somewhat by placing earthworm bins under the cages). The rabbits get sore feet from the wire mesh, and often become so nervous that they kill their new-born young. How would you like it if you were still a half-wild baboon in a cramped cage, with a tiger staring at you face to face from a foot away?

Rabbits can be raised in a shed and outdoor run much like that described for chickens, with a good tight mesh fence. Rabbits, even wild ones, really don't get through or under fences very often, contrary to the Peter Rabbit tales. My grandfather raised rabbits in his orchard, letting the hoppers run free there. When he wanted *hassenpfeffer* for dinner, he shot a couple.

For many years, I thought this was just another example of the aberrant behavior characteristic of my family, but pasture-raised rabbits recently came into the farm news again. It seems that Joel Salatin, the contrary farmer mentioned earlier, was raising rabbits with his brother by grazing them on pastures in movable pens (like Chicken Tractors). Salatin found that the method worked just fine, and he used the idea not only for rabbits, but to launch his now famous pastured chicken enterprise.

You can adopt the bare bones of this method and raise rabbits in your yard the way ranchers raise beef in Nebraska, with the humbler goal of roasted rabbit for dinner occasionally. In a yard pen, where you should grow white clover for the rabbits to graze, you can let the buck run with the herd. You can place little hutches on the ground (5- or 10-gallon kegs, buckets, or barrels laid on their sides, stabilized with rocks or stakes, work fine) for them to nest in, with some brushy or leafy shelter for cover, or you can feed them in a little shed, like hens, and they will come in regularly to eat if they have been penned in for a week or so. With nest boxes on the floor, mother rabbits will pull the fur from under their chin to make a soft nest lining, and they'll have their young in these boxes, usually with much less trouble than in cramped cages. The fence around the pen needs to be as tall as for a calf, 36 inches anyway, because domestic rabbits can leap like Olympic highjumpers if a dog starts barking at them. The fence keeps dogs out, too. We used to feed our rabbits oats and yard grass/hay. You can grow a patch of oats in the garden and start feeding the rabbits with oats, stalks and all, from the time the grain is in the milky stage. Or move the rabbits into the oats. Clover cut, dried, and nice and green, is almost a complete food for them, but of course they enjoy carrots and other garden vegetables. In early spring they appreciate tree prunings to gnaw on. Domestic "yard" rabbits, being much prettier and more imposing than wild ones, are pleasurable to look at hopping on the grass of their grazing lot, and add to the charm of your garden bestiary. You can move the fence pen around like the Salatins do, to let the rabbits mow-graze parts of the lawn. If a rabbit does escape and joins the wild fraternity, what's one more rabbit in the neighborhood?

Of course, there is no good reason why you should not think of the wild rabbits feasting on your garden produce as part of your livestock. You feed them. Eat them, too.

## Earthworms

Twenty-five years ago, earthworm hustlers engineered a pyramid scam that left thousands of people who had invested in backyard "worm farms" with lots of worms but no place to market them. That situation, says Clive Edwards, a scientist at Ohio State who has spent a large part of his life studying earthworms, actually led to a positive rebirth of interest in earthworms because all those people wanted to know if there was any honest way to salvage some of their losses.

These days, the waste recycling industry is turning seriously to the use of earthworms in processing yardwaste and foodwaste into compost.

"Commercial vermiculture as an industry in itself is beginning to mature," says *BioCycle* magazine, a leading publication in the recycling industry that is headquartered in Emmaus, Pennsylvania. For example, Oregon Soil Corporation, near Portland, has been processing five tons of food scraps, two tons of yard trimmings, and a half a ton of paper into compost every day with earthworms. Dan Holcombe, who runs the operation on an organic vegetable farm, is quoted in *BioCycle* saying, "I've never seen any mechanical technology do a better job of composting waste than the earthworms themselves."

"Vermicomposting" technology came directly from backyard gardening, through the efforts of people like Mary Appelhof, a vivacious and tireless gardener who lives in Kalamazoo, Michigan. She has made the popularization of earthworms as garbage recyclers and garden fertilizers her life's work. (Her book, *Worms Eat My Garbage,* the sprightliest and most understandable guide to raising earthworms, is available from her Flower Press, 10332 Shaver Road, Kalamazoo, Michigan 49002.) To doubters who say earthworms are too slow for large municipal composting, she will reply with great vigor that if enough people would use worms to take care of their own garbage, there wouldn't be a need for so many large, expensive, municipal composting systems.

Essentially, Mary tells me, all you do is:

1. Get a box, wood or plastic.
2. Fill it with shredded corrugated cardboard (which works best) or animal manure, peat moss, shredded leaves, newspaper, a little soil, and a tiny bit of agricultural lime.
3. Dampen and add redworms (nightcrawlers don't work well).
4. Add a shallow layer of food wastes every day. A pound of worms will handle a half pound of food wastes a day.
5. Remove increase of worms to start more boxes, for fish bait, for feeding as protein to chickens, or to put in the garden.
6. Remove composted castings for fertilizer.

It is almost as easy as it sounds. If you want a biology project for children, Mary tells me that raising worms on food waste is very popular in schools. The children can do it all. They make up the worm bins, put in the worms, feed them food waste from the cafeteria, and grow more food in a school garden using the worm compost for fertilizer.

Earthworms are of particular importance to me as fish food. My mulch beds are actually my worm bins, or perhaps more accurately, my worm pasture. I can easily grub a half a jar of worms from under the mulch every day to feed my fish. In the web of life that extends ultimately to my stomach, the worms nourish the vegetables I eat, and then they nourish the fish I eat, and if I am buried the way I want to be buried, I will then nourish the worms.

# CHAPTER 8

# PROTECTING THE GARDEN
# FROM THE WILD EMPIRE

Gandhi posed this question: If a poisonous snake is about to bite me, should I allow myself to be bitten, or should I kill it, supposing that there is no other way in which I can save myself? The Jain teacher, Raychandbhai Mehta, answered that a person of highest virtue, as he assumed Gandhi aspired to be, would endure the snakebite rather than kill the snake.

Include me out. I am evidently not a person of highest virtue, though I admire Gandhi tremendously. First of all, there always are other alternatives in this dilemma, but if not, it's goodbye snake where I come from. I bet that if Gandhi were ever in the position of having to make that choice, he'd goodbye the snake, too. I'll bet even money that Mehta would, too.

On the other hand, Harlan Hubbard (see chapter 2) did practice the kind of forbearance that the Jains championed, sort of. On my last visit to see him, he was in the hospital, recovering from a copperhead bite. He was remarkably composed about the ordeal, and showed no hostility at all toward the snake. "I knew that copperhead lived under the rocks of our walk," he said. "I had no business going out there after dark in my bare feet." He gave no indication that he intended to get rid of the snake when he returned home. His only resolve was to wear shoes outside at night from then on.

Harlan's philosophy helps me come to terms with a dilemma that I can't completely solve for myself: I hate to kill anything, but sometimes I am convinced that I must. I will "wear shoes" when that kind of alternative choice will suffice to save wildlife and me, but I will kill when I think I have to. We allowed hornets to build one of their huge ovoid nests on our porch once (they kill flies), something that horrified our sidewalk-environmentalist friends, who pretended to be shocked when I killed a raccoon that had emptied the eggs out of a bluebird nest.

I do not believe in letting nature take its course all the time. In a world where one ethnic group of Rwandans hacked a million people of another ethnic group to death with machetes recently, I don't have the time nor the luxury to debate whether I should kill a feral cat that is endangering a rare species of songbird. To make the point clearly, if I were a judge, I could sentence a vicious human criminal to death under the law—with fewer qualms than I feel when killing a poor dumb pest animal, which is merely the victim of a situation that is as much my fault, as a human, as the animal's fault. But in either case I would act, not lie down passively and let someone else make the decision. If this sounds unconscionably brutal to you, try arguing the passive-resistance viewpoint with a brood of termites under your house or a panther eyeing up your child.

The sidewalk environmentalists who pretend to be shocked at the killing of pestiferous wildlife, or of domestic animals raised for meat, display an attitude that I think confuses rather than helps our collective environmental dismay. The way of nature is to eat and be eaten. The only unnatural death in nature is a natural death. For modern human society to deny this fundamental law of nature is an indication of how far we have been able to remove ourselves from the real world. This attitude is especially irresponsible when it is coupled, as it so often is, with an insistence that humans have the "right" to go on increasing our own populations without limits.

To show just how relentlessly complicated and unsolvable is the issue of "animal rights" from the viewpoint of letting nature take its course, consider the status of deer. The white-tailed deer is statistically the deadliest animal to humans (and to many species of tree seedlings). Some one hundred and twenty people nationally die every year by way of deer-car accidents. In Ohio alone in 1995, deer were involved in twenty-four thousand road collisions. You can argue that human population is as much to blame as the deer population for this dilemma, and I would agree, but nevertheless the fact remains: Those cute deer are far more of a menace than rattlesnakes or man-eating tigers. In addition, there are some ten thousand new cases of Lyme disease reported every year, spread to humans by the deer tick.

But while Eastern states lament their high deer populations, Californians are lamenting too many mountain lions killing too many deer to suit the hunters. Mountain lions need to die anyway, say some, because they kill a human (on very rare occasions). So we have a situation in which mountain lions are "worse" than deer, even though mountain lions are much, much less life-threatening to people.

Pursue the debate a little farther into absurdity. The ecologist would say that the mountain lion is the proper solution for keeping the deer population in check, and I agree. So by the same logic, why is not the mountain lion a proper solution for helping at least now and then to keep the human population in check?

How we solve the cultural issue of letting nature take its course is most important to backyard food production, because the biggest threat to gardening success in these modern times—as amazing as it may seem to the uninitiated—is not bugs, disease, weeds, bad weather, or poor soil, but wild animals. Certain species are overpopulating dangerously, as a direct result of society's seemingly humane but unsustainable philosophy of abnegating its responsibilities for husbandry. I would not be surprised to see commercial agribusiness join hands with the sidewalk environmentalists in denouncing those of us who kill rabbits, raccoons, deer, squirrels, chipmunks, English sparrows, feral dogs and cats, armadillos, groundhogs, gophers, moles, Canada geese, and Norway rats—along with chickens, hogs, cows, and goats. We are agribusiness's biggest competitor, and if we could be discouraged from cottage food production, society would become dependent on agrifacturing's assembly-line meat and irradiated vegetables.

Agribusiness won't ever join sidewalk environmentalism, of course, because the wild empire hurts agribusiness profits even more than we contrary gardeners do. The Farm Bureau (which cries for getting the government out of farming out of one side of its mouth, and whines for government help out of the other), says that deer alone cause millions and millions of dollars in damages to farm crops. Deer are a serious enough problem that the organization makes them one of its major lobbying issues (not because it cares that much about farmers, but because the Farm Bureau is in the insurance business, and deer are wrecking the auto-insurance racket). *Farm Journal* magazine reported in its March 1992 issue that for agriculture, "the price tag for feeding the nation's deer herd alone could exceed $1 *billion* a year."

Spoiled Americans dismiss the problem of food losses to wild animals because for fifty years we have enjoyed food surpluses (though many people around the world still don't get enough to eat). Only in 1996, after three years of declining grain supplies worldwide together with climbing populations, did we realize how close to food shortages the world hovers.

Wild-animal overpopulations are even more of a threat to other species of wildlife than they are to humans. For instance, ornithologists say that cowbirds are killing off wood thrushes, and I take this personally because no music, not Beethoven nor the Beatles, equals thrush song at eventide. Cowbirds lay their eggs in other bird's nests, and are increasing in numbers because human activity has been leveling woodland in favor of grain fields. When I find a baby cowbird in a chipping-sparrow nest, hogging all the food Mother Sparrow brings for her brood, I feed the cowbird to the cat.

I don't know where the anthropomorphic notion of virtuous animals got started. I have watched English sparrows slaughter cliff-swallow nestlings, not to eat nor to use the nest, but, I swear, out of a deliberate instinct for murder. The kindliest man I know kills every English sparrow that comes on his farm, because otherwise his cliff swallows would soon be gone.

You say that I am being just as anthropocentric in my view of wildlife as the let-nature-take-its-course advocates are in theirs? I say that after having turned the wild world upside-down through our own burgeoning populations and technologies, humans must make knowledgeable efforts to keep the ecological theater of life open to all species. By our very presence on Earth, we cannot *not* act in its management. I prefer, therefore, to do this management as rationally as the best available biological knowledge allows—not by the whimsical, soft, Rousseauvian philosophy of letting nature take its course, nor by metaphysical passivity. How can we, as the Gaian theorists evidently pretend to believe, attribute some grand and mysterious intelligence to rocks and trees and oceans, while denigrating human intelligence, without which we could never arrive at such outlandish conclusions?

There is a very dangerous attitude developing among ecological thinkers, even among those I treasure as comrades and friends. In reaction to the scientific reductionism that has lorded over the Western world with such disgusting hubris for over a hundred years, a necessary counterattack is being launched. But this counterattack is going to the opposite extreme: It would toss aside the sanctity of human reason in favor of emotional and mystical thinking. We don't know enough to make judgments about managing nature, says this philosophy. Then its practitioners proceed to pontificate on nature with a hubris far more arrogant than that of science.

Passivity is not possible in our situation. We cannot pass the buck by saying that truth is ultimately unknowable. Any posture of *not* managing the earth is, in fact, a method of managing it. Moreover, an excess of emotional or mystical fervor in management is just as bad as an excess of rationalism. To deny that humans are rational (as often as I am tempted to do so) is to open the floodgates of chaos. Then every wacko in the country will step forward, offering an unending parade of self-glorifying and emotional superstitions as the answer to our problems.

We must pick and choose our way along a path we do not know enough about, that is for sure, like crossing a river over half-submerged stepping-stones. Personal, concrete, local, *rational* experience, backed by *rational* study of what facts and theories are known about population dynamics, must be our pervading guide. We must try to find a middle road between Descartes and Rousseau. I don't mind an owl or hawk taking one of my chickens occasionally, since invariably they will get that old biddy who is most infirmed by age anyway, and besides, a couple of my chickens are more expendable than the owls and hawks on my farm. But raccoons, always on the verge of overpopulation leading to death from distemper or rabies anyway, will kill every hen in the coop, not out of hunger but just out of a kind of manic delirium. I don't intend to let this happen on my farm.

Feral cats are decimating the ranks of beneficial songbirds. These cats are a problem resulting directly from human activity (or rather inactivity), and must be solved by human activity. The way you solve a feral-cat problem is to kill the sonuvabitch. Likewise, overpopulations of Canada geese are a human-caused problem and must become a human-solved problem. Having too many squirrels in towns also results from human ordinances, and the problem must be solved by countervailing human ordinances.

Unmanaged deer populations threaten many kinds of plant life, and then die of starvation anyway. Deer are making the establishment of new hardwood forests in certain areas nearly impossible, and none of those sprays and ointments that are supposed to discourage them work reliably when the deer are starving (see Bob Chenoweth's interesting book *Black Walnut*, Sagamore, 1995). I know from observation that hungry, over-populating deer are eating wild trillium, one of our loveliest, and in some places endangered, wildflowers. Rather than see the trillium destroyed, I encourage hunters on my property to kill the excess deer.

Deer will eat almost all garden vegetables except tomatoes and other species of the Solanum family, and they might eat even these when hungry enough. To my knowledge, deer do not eat daffodils, delphiniums, irises, annual poppies, or impatiens. But heaven help most other flowers. Whatever you plant in deer-protected suburban enclaves, do not choose hosta lilies. A white-tailed deer will seek out this landscape flower even right under your picture window, and if you decide to argue, it may panic and jump through the glass. A deer crashed into a church window in our town last fall: the joke going around was that it was after the hostas on the altar.

Gene Gerue, whose sprightly and practical *How to Find Your Ideal*

*Country Home* (Heartwood Publications, HC 78, Box 1105, Zanoni, MO 65784) makes good reading for contrary gardeners, tells me that in the wilder parts of the Ozarks, where he lives, he has been forced to give up gardening almost entirely or build some very tall, strong fences. "There are twelve does and last-year fawns eating acorns in the yard right now," he told me during a phone conversation recently.

Wild animals are now becoming a serious urban problem as well. And here is one farmer and gardener who is laughing like hell as I watch pretentious urban nature-lovers suddenly change their minds when the depredations hit their property. Some of the very same people who fought and won a battle to ban deer hunting in their suburban sanctuaries in and around Lyme, Connecticut, went to the opposite extreme and became advocates of killing all the deer in Christendom after a dangerous disease, carried by deer ticks, became so prevalent there that it was named after the town. Bambi ain't so cute in Lyme anymore. "The pattern repeats itself almost exactly in every metro area that has a deer problem," says John Daugherty of the Division of Wildlife in Ohio. "First, everyone wants the deer around. As deer numbers increase, so do deer problems, and people start shouting at each other about what to do. Inevitably the deer begin to starve, and after costly and ineffective efforts to remove them to other places, city officials are forced to reach a decision: Maintain the park deer herd at a certain level and 'harvest' the rest." (Our ambivalent society can't bring itself to use the world "kill" in reference to wildlife, although it seems okay to say "kill" when referring to Iraqis or Jordanians.)

The same turnaround is occurring with Canada geese. Now that these flying manure-spreaders are overrunning golf courses, city parks, and small town reservoirs, they don't seem as majestically beautiful as they once did. In response to crescendoing complaints, some state departments of natural resources are extending the goose-hunting season and allowing property owners to break eggs in goose nests as a way to control population. Again I say that it is a strange society that approves of breaking eggs in a nest, but not killing Mother Goose and giving the meat to hungry people.

The days of amiable Ranger Rick are over. Yet it seems to take a calamity to teach people the proper lessons in population dynamics. Recurring epidemics of rabies have been plaguing the Eastern part of the nation in recent years, but you don't hear much about this because authorities don't want to "unduly alarm the people." In New York and Pennsylvania, a thousand people had to endure the arduous rabies treatment in 1993 through 1994, and while only one human death from rabies was recorded during that time (and seems to have been contracted in another country), thousands of animals bitten by rabid raccoons and other infected mammals died. The stricken raccoons died too, of course—one of nature's ways of reducing overpopulation.

Around our farm, the raccoon population finally reached such a high level—partly because coon hunting and trapping are now politically incorrect—that distemper swept through, as it always will, and trimmed the ranks. In Yuppieland, distemper is okay; trapping is bad.

It takes little imagination to liken the rampage of overpopulated wildlife to a war, led by the redoubtable General Rac Coon (formerly Ranger Rick). My state, Ohio, is apparently at the center of the battle. The Raccoon Surveillance Program (yes, really), implemented by the Division of Wildlife and the Department of Health, admits that it can't stop the invading armies, but must rely on natural controls such as distemper for defense. From the East, black bears have joined the coons, boldly storming into villages, looting trash cans and landfills in broad daylight. A pincer movement of coyotes and wild dogs proceeds from the West, killing about a thousand sheep per year. From the North, squadrons of Canada geese strafe golf courses, farm ponds, lawns, and wheat fields, turning turf into quagmires. Commando squirrels aid the offensive by chewing through electric lines on utility poles, disrupting communications. Zebra mussels plug the water intakes of nuclear power plants on Lake Erie (I am *not* kidding), threatening shutdowns. In southern Ohio, woodpeckers drill holes in house walls. Earwigs have gone on a reign of terror in Columbus, even chasing people from their beds. (Nope, still not kidding.) Rabbits, reminiscent of Sherman's march to the sea, systematically lay waste to all the unfenced suburban gardens between Bellevue and Lake Erie. (Some slight exaggeration here, but not much.) And most destructive of all, kamikaze deer hurl themselves in front of automobiles and through picture windows and plate-glass storefronts. Not long ago, two deer even penetrated a *downtown* parking garage in Cleveland; nobody knows how they got there.

Why are so many species of wildlife on a population rampage? Humans (who, don't forget, are on a similar rampage) unwittingly provide nearly perfect habitat for them (although the parking garage hardly fits that description). We now have acres and acres of land held by investors around cities for future development. This land is growing up in brush—deer and groundhog heaven. At the same time, acres of pastureland, too hilly or costly for tractors to cultivate, are returning to brush and woodland as livestock farmers cram their animals into confined factory buildings. Both New England and Ohio have more wooded acreage today (albeit of far poorer quality) than they did a century ago, in part because so many family farms have failed. To complement all this cover, vast grain farms provide an almost unlimited banquet table for some wildlife. Coons didn't try to tear my corn crib down this winter, for a change, because ears of corn littered a nearby field due to an improperly operated mechanical harvester.

Studies in Eastern and Midwestern states show that raccoons are now more densely established in cities and suburbs than in rural areas. The masked bandits find plenty of den sites in mature trees, the kind lovingly protected in cities but ruthlessly cut for lumber in the country. Unmaintained attics and abandoned buildings, especially old barns left when the tide of housing development rolls over an area, also make wonderful homes for raccoons (and groundhogs). They travel via storm sewer and culvert, safe from dogs, and sally forth to raid garbage cans, gardens, and pet's dishes. Raccoons are a great boon to the pet-food industry; in many cases, they steal more than the pets eat.

Typical of our society's deep ignorance about wildlife is the current practice of live-trapping animals in town and transferring them to the country. This is no kinder, gentler a way than the equally irresponsible practice of abandoning kittens and puppies in the countryside to get rid of them because the owners are too lazy to care for them, too yellow-bel-lied to kill them, or too busy to take them to the local humane society (where they will be killed if no one adopts them). Purveyors of cage traps play up to the kinder, gentler myth in their ads. "Trap wild animals hu-manely, then release them far away," says one catalog. Far away? *Where* is far away? In the countryside, where we already have more pest animals than nature can support? "Transferring animals to another environment is not humane," says John Daugherty, the wildlife scientist quoted earlier in this chapter. "Studies show that in some cases, as many as 90 percent of the raccoons transferred out of town succumb to raccoons already territorially established there." In fact, Ohio's Department of Natural Resources is moving toward making the transferral of trapped animals il-legal. We country gardeners, who bare the brunt of this irresponsible practice, breathe a sigh of relief.

The cage trap is, incidentally, an excellent way to control certain pest animals, especially raccoons, groundhogs, and chipmunks. The models that have only one entrance, with the bait placed at the other end, are *much* better than those with an entrance at each end and the bait trigger or treadle in the middle. Get the larger size designated for raccoons, as it will catch the smaller pests, too. I have found it particularly effective to place concrete blocks or chunks of wood outside the bait end of the cage on all three sides and on top of the trap, so as to encourage the animal to enter the other end rather than stand outside at the rear and try to reach its paws in to the bait. Coons will also learn how to upset the trap so the bait falls through the screening. When I can find a raccoon trail (oh yes, they will make well-defined paths from the woods to your garden—that's how many of them are out there) that goes through a woven wire fence, I set the trap with the entrance opening right at the fence. Accustomed to going through the fence anyway, the raccoon will often go into the cage without hesitation.

The advantage of a cage trap is that if you catch a pet or a wild ani-mal that is either beneficial or not causing a problem,you can release it. For example, opossums are plentiful here, but not troublesome—in fact, like hedgehogs in England, they benefit the garden by eating pest bugs and rodents. Release opossums, please, unless you are sure you have an overpopulation of them. Skunks also should ordinarily not be killed, because they are largely beneficial. They control ground wasps fairly well, for one thing, digging up the nests and eating the larvae. Skunks have the run of our place, and we have had no problems with them other than a little odor on a few warm spring nights. Skunks are quite amusing to watch, and are very tolerant of humans because they know they have the upperhand. They can contract rabies, but rarely do.

However, how a person would release a skunk from a cage trap is beyond me. I have tried to figure out a way to make a very long wire release for the trap, but have not been successful. Wildlife handlers say they can throw a blanket over the whole cage trap, then quietly open the door for the skunk to exit. Fortunately, I have never caught a skunk, and I never set the trap where I know skunks frequent.

There is no humane way to kill anything. Here again we enter into another absurdity, as animal lovers argue among themselves over how to kill unwanted dogs and cats. The People for the Ethical Treatment of Animals (PETA) recently sued the Columbiana County, Ohio, county commissioners over the way the dog pound was killing stray dogs. The dog pound was using a "homemade" carbon monoxide system, while PETA insisted on lethal injections. Anything homemade is suspect today, I guess, but anyone who thinks carbon monoxide is a worse way to kill a dog than a lethal injection really has me baffled. Considering the alternatives at my disposal, I think drowning is the most merciful method of execution. I drop the cage trap, animal inside, into the rainbarrel or into the creek. I suppose others could argue that a bullet in the head is quicker, but what if the bullet only wounds the animal?

People also refuse to believe what I know: that animals do not feel pain as humans do. This spring, one of our lambs developed a large tumor in its scrotum. Really gross. I was tempted to put the creature out of its misery, but it was bouncing jauntily around the pasture like the other lambs. We decided to let the veterinarian operate. He removed the entire scrotum and sewed the lamb back up at one in the afternoon. We took the lamb home three hours later and turned it loose in the pasture.

Away it ran, as fast and as carefree as a healthy lamb, bleating until it found its mother, and then nursed vigorously. Can you imagine a human recovering that fast without painkillers? Even with painkillers?

The lack of a sense of husbandry is apparent in the way so many humans shirk their responsibilities as pet owners. They think pets are toys. They refuse to have their toys neutered, and then let them run loose and breed. The young go wild, or are given up to the animal shelter or the dog warden, who must find homes for them or kill them. The National Humane Society says about half the dogs and cats it takes in must be "euthanized" (note again the reluctance to say "killed"). Estimates of the number so killed every year vary from 6 million to as high as 20 million. In addition, the number of uncaptured dogs and cats running wild because of human irresponsibility is inestimable, and they kill countless numbers of beneficial birds and other animals.

Even domestic cats take a terrible toll on native ground-nesting birds. Wildlife scientists have calculated, based on a Wisconsin study, that domestic cats kill 19 million songbirds nationwide every year. Putting a bell on the cat does not work. Feeding the cat well does not stop it. Declawing the cat will do no good. The only effective way to stop this killing, say the experts, is to keep the cat confined, at least during nesting season.

Of course, with powerful logic I might argue that the whole wildlife "problem" is only correctable by limiting the number of people in the world. Hush your mouth, you naughty boy.

It seems to me that the only fruitful way to discuss the thorny problem of managing nature is to require everyone to do some serious gardening or farming before being allowed to debate the topic. If everyone had to produce at least a little food before buying any more food, the let-nature-take-its-course philosophy would quickly vanish. Everyone would then understand what it means to deal with nature in the concrete, not the abstract. Whatever our beliefs before gardening or farming, they will change after experience tempers either a previously naive love of nature or a previously fearful dislike of nature. Something more practical, in the emotional and intellectual middle, will take center stage in how we define "living in harmony with nature." Can anything live in harmony with what it eats? Can the fox live in harmony with the hens?

Gardening in harmony with nature requires a much broader view of life than just knowing and practicing the organic how-to's of protecting domestic plants and animals from their wild predators, and vice versa. The overall basic how-to is to try to understand how a garden or farm is connected ecologically with its surrounding environs, not isolated in a backyard or within fences. The first deduction you can then make is that as humans advance their living space in the usual ways, their cities, suburbs, farms, highways, and other developments destroy habitat (food and shelter) for some wildlife and enhance habitat for other wildlife. Both the so-called Bambi lovers and the so-called NRA gun lovers agree with the truth of this deduction, I think. I think they also agree with what ecologists now know more or less for certain: Habitat preservation is the key to wildife sustainability. With enough food and shelter to reproduce healthfully, wildife can endure surprisingly high levels of predation and human interference. Groundhogs were literally undermining the runways at Columbus International Airport a few years ago, oblivious to the noise. They had all the food they needed, a place to dig, and no predators. Loss of habitat, on the other hand, reduces wildife populations much more severely than hunters and trappers do. For example, in the southeastern United States, there is plenty of more or less wild land, empty of humans, where the ivory-billed woodpecker used to proliferate, but drainage and logging took away the particular kind of wetland and old-growth forest community that the bird needed, and so now it is very rare and may be extinct.

Humans can remedy the situation significantly if we as a society view our living places, including our cities, as habitat for the greatest possible *diversity* of wildlife, and if we then take it upon ourselves to keep in check the number of those species prone to overpopulation because of us. This means not only putting up bluebird houses, but trapping and killing raccoons. If doing so leads to too many bluebirds and not enough raccoons, then we should turn the management process around. We have long passed the time when we can just let nature take its course. By our own willingness to increase our human population, along with our food supply and our ability to live longer, we are not letting nature take its course in the first place.

Gardening lends itself to a goal of increasing diversity of species, and is directly benefitted by it. In terms of avoiding wild animal predations, the best places to garden are not in towns, where certain kinds of wildlife can build up hungry and unnaturally large populations, nor out in the wilderness, where large populations of wild animals presumably occur naturally. The best-protected garden spots are in places where intensive but intelligent farming and hunting and trapping are practiced. Intelligent farming will see to it that a varied habitat has been maintained for a very diverse number of species with a very diverse choice of food to eat, while intelligent hunting and trapping will have kept those species that are prone to population explosions at an acceptable level relative to the other species.

Out here in contrary-farmer country, we try very hard to foster as many wildlife habitats as possible (creek, pond, woodland, meadow, orchard, garden, wetland, rotated grain plots), while trying equally hard to limit the population of those species able to take too much advantage of a humanized landscape. We do not have nearly the problems of protecting our garden food supply as our friends in town do. Some of us put up electric fences around our corn patches to protect them against deer, raccoons, and groundhogs, or low chicken-wire fences around peas and beans to protect them against rabbits, but our son in a village and our daughter in the suburb of a large city have to fence and screen *everything*. Without adequate wild food sources to turn to, out of control populations prey hungrily upon almost all the vegetables and fruits our son and daughter plant. Flocks of English sparrows and starlings riddle peas. Robins make fruit-growing impossible, and netting is only partially effective. Without wild nut trees to turn to, squirrels and chipmunks take to raiding the garden and fruit trees, and are almost impossible to screen out. Without wild clovers (killed by lawn sprays) to fill up on, rabbits chew just about anything that grows. Not helping matters, regular public spraying for mosquitoes kills beneficial insects as well, and reduces the whole insect food chain that otherwise would not only help keep pest insect populations in check, but also would supply alternative provender for pestiferous birds.

A town or suburb or farm needs to see itself as part of a wildlife preserve, and the whole community should cooperate in establishing an extended environment of lovely diversity. A garden in every backyard would be a giant-sized first step. Even one in every third backyard would be nice, if all contained a large diversity of foods, not just five tomato plants each.

Urban tree plantings ought to be guided by the broad ecological view, as is now becoming the case in progressive communities, so that the trees together form an urban forest habitat for all native wildlife species. Trees makes good economic sense, too. According to S. R. Templeton and G. Goldman of the Department of Agriculture at UC–Berkeley, urban forestry adds $3.8 billion to the California economy from the ripple effects of $1.2 billion worth of tree product sales; sixty-four thousand jobs; and about $1 billion worth of aesthetic, recreational, and environmental benefits.

By the same token, all farms ought to have a woodlot of native species, or plots of native prairie and wetland. Portions of backyards and town parks ought to be mowed only once a year, or once every other year, to allow a growth of tall grass and brush, protecting garter snakes, toads, and grassland birds that prey on harmful insects. Barn-owl houses ought to be built atop appropriate public buildings to encourage this predator of rats and mice, and every backyard ought to have a screech-owl house, if hollow trees don't provide them naturally. (A goodly portion of the human population still believes that owls signal the approach of death in human households. This is what happens when you deny rationality.) Garden pools for aquatic life ought to be a part of every larger backyard. Those huge, manicured lawns we see around factories and business offices especially could be utilized in such ways.

Eventually, we could turn our towns, suburbs, and farms into extremely pleasant natural preserves, where we could see from our kitchen and office windows as much wildlife as we can now enjoy in a national park. And if, occasionally, some species of wildlife becomes too numerous in relation to the others, have a feast!

Sally Fallon (in *Nourishing Traditions,* cited in chapters 6 and 7) does not laugh at my suggestions of eating common wildlife. She sends me a recipe for opossum or coon from her friend Tommy Strawther, who lives on a farm in Karnak, Texas. It goes like this:

"Singe hairs off possum until the hide is as smooth as the back of your hand. Then wash. Skin a coon. After butchering, soak in vinegar overnight. Then boil meat over low flame until tender. Boil in favorite vegetable seasonings such as celery, bell peppers, onions, etc. Use other seasonings to taste as well, such as garlic powder, onion powder, seasoning salt, etc. Remove from boiler after desired tenderness. Place in roast pan with cooked vegetables. Cut sweet potatoes to desired size or slice. Place potatoes around meat. Pour broth around potatoes. Cover. Slow bake at 300 degrees [Fahrenheit] for about one hour or until meat is as brown as desired. . . .

"As for small animals [she had not altogether jokingly mentioned *taupe en daube*—mole stew], they can be fixed in a manner similar to my recipe for wild duck stew. They should be cut in pieces, marinated in wine, vinegar, or lemon juice for twenty-four hours (in fridge), dried well, dredged in flour, browned in fat (duck fat), and cooked in broth with garden vegetables and herbs. Sauce can be thickened with arrowroot [a waterside plant that can be grown easily at the edge of your garden pool]."

I know a family who uses a similar recipe for squirrels and rabbits, and cooks them all up in a huge iron kettle over an open fire. They call it Hunter's Stew. It's delicious, especially after waiting an hour or two for it to cook until tender while standing near the beer keg.

## Selected Pest Controls

To keep the killing of wild animals at a minimum, or avoid it altogether, here is a selected list of pest controls that my sixty years of experience have found worth repeating.

## Walls and Fences

A solid rock or brick wall around your garden, high enough (seven feet) so a deer can't see over it (they won't jump where they can't see) and so even a squirrel or raccoon finds it hard to climb, is the surest way not to have to share your garden with nightly visitors. The wall should have a footer at least twelve inches deep underneath to discourage moles and groundhogs from digging their way in. Yes, this is the expensive way to go, but Scott and Helen Nearing built such a wall around their garden, and they were not the kind of people to ever waste a cent on extravagance. A masonry wall also reduces wind chill and wind damage considerably in the garden, and acts as a heat sink to protect plants close to it from late frost. It also provides ultimate privacy for those who like to bask in the sun without fear of prying neighborhood eyes. For the same reason, a walled garden makes a grand place for observing or photographing wildlife outside the garden. You can peer over the top, or through an opening near the top, and not spook wild animals.

The only other more or less foolproof barrier is an electric fence. The ideal kind, in my estimation, is electrified netting that you can stretch around your garden fast and easily, such as Electroguard and Electronet from Premier Fence Company in Washington, Iowa (other manufacturers make similar products). For deer, some companies offer electrified tape strands that are easy for the deer to see before they barge through. The idea is that they will smell the tape first and bingo, never come back again. Some wildlife experts say that dangling a few pieces of metal covered with peanut butter on the electrified wire tempts the deer to take a lick, and then they get a lick of watts and ohms that they do not soon forget. Deer managers also say that a double fence, about six feet apart, electrified or not, will deter deer. The thinking is that they may be high jumpers but not broad jumpers. I do not agree. I think one eight-foot fence is better than two five-footers, and takes up less room in your yard.

The best tall fence barrier for deer, in my opinion, is heavy-gauge, rigid wire gates that farmers use to make pens for sheep and hogs. This rigid fencing comes in various panel lengths and heights, up to sixteen feet long and five or six feet tall. The advantage of making a fence out of this material is that you don't need to stretch it tight; it is already rigid. It is too expensive to use for fencing fields or large lots, but justifiable for smallish gardens. If the panels are four feet high, you need to stack three atop one another to gain the desired twelve feet. You might get away with going only nine feet or even seven feet high. I have learned not to make rules where deer are concerned. Do seven-footers first, and if deer jump it, go higher. Don't forget to make a gate into the garden. This type of fence is not particularly attractive, but it is long-lasting. Trellis your tomatoes on it; I don't think the deer will eat them.

## Screening

Screening some plants can be effective. It helps to build a frame of 2 x 4s over your blueberry and raspberry bushes and grapevines, and cover the frame with screening, but this is laborious and expensive and high maintenance. Birds and raccoons can devise a score of ways to penetrate the screen, besides. Make sure it is far enough away from the fruit so predators can't reach your crop through the screening. Netting draped over strawberry beds helps only a little, because birds learn to land on the netting and poke the berries through it. If you have a selection of different fruits and a selection of different birds, all keeping any one species from hogging the environment of your garden, they will eat only some of the strawberries, cherries, mulberries, and so on, and leave enough for you. Over the course of the season, our fruit-eating birds enjoy juneberries, wild and tame strawberries, cherries, early apples, wild and tame raspberries, blackberries, gooseberries, elderberries, more apples, peaches, pears, wild black cherries, pokeberries, crab apples, hawthorn apples, osier dogwood berries, common dogwood berries, wild rose hips, the infernal multiflora rose hips, autumn olive berries, juniper berries, poison-ivy berries, and (if they get real hungry) bittersweet berries. That table of fare sort of keeps the opposition disorganized. If you like cherries, plant two full-sized trees. Then, in good cherry years, there will be enough for the birds to gorge on early, leaving you plenty of the ripest, sweetest fruit later on. Yes, really. In poor cherry years, leash a cat to a clothesline near the tree. The robins get so busy cussing the cat that they don't get so many cherries eaten.

*Pest-Resistant Planting*

Buy apple trees that are immune to scab, to ward off this most treacherous "wild" threat in humid climates to a good pie. 'Liberty' is the best variety so far, in my opinion. Without having to worry about scab, you don't have to spray unless you are in the commercial business of selling apples. Make cider of apples that aren't cosmetically perfect. Keep trying different varieties until you find some that will produce fairly well without spraying. I have found that since I refuse to spray at all, I have fewer bugs in general. Yes, really. My 'Liberty', 'Virginia Winesap', 'Yellow Delicious', and several wild apple trees I found in old fence rows seem less affected by insects, and show at least some resistance to scab.

I grow peaches now in a sort of opening in the woods next to the chicken coop. The woodland trees protect somewhat against late frosts, and the hens do a better job of controlling borers than I ever did with organic defenses such as ashes around the trunks.

*Birdhouses*

To prevent buildups of pest insects, reduce their habitat and increase the habitat of their enemies. In towns and suburbs, mosquitoes mostly breed in water standing in plugged roof spouting. Provide birdhouses aplenty around your garden for insect-eating birds. Gourds make great houses for wrens and purple martins, two of the very best bug-catchers. Grow the gourds. Let them overwinter in a dry place. In spring, cut a hole the desired size (one-inch diameter for wrens, one and a half inches for bluebirds, and two and a half inches for martins) in the side with a pocketknife, and empty out the seeds inside. Run a wire through the stem end and hang the gourdhouse on a tree limb.

For purple martins, buy two lengths of plastic drainpipe each about twelve feet long, one a size smaller than the other so that it slips inside the other. Set the larger pipe in the ground as you would a post, putting gravel around it in the hole, and tamp solidly. Toward the top of that pipe, cut several holes about six inches apart that will take a half-inch bolt. Next, drill several matching holes in the bottom end of the other pipe. Slide the second pipe inside the first. The upper pipe can be raised until the holes in both coincide. Slide a bolt through—voilà, a cheap stand for a martin house. When you want to take it down, pull out the bolt and let the top pipe slide down.

Use large gourds for the martin houses themselves. To hang the gourds, drill three sets of holes in the top of the top pipe, at different angles from one another and at slightly different heights. Slide three wooden bars (broomsticks will work) or three quarter-inch plastic pipes about three feet long each through the three sets of holes, and then hang gourdhouses on the bars—as many as four per bar, two on each side of the center pipe. This gives you a total of twelve houses, with the opportunity to add more. Very simple. Because the gourds are light, no other pole support is needed. Whether you get martins or not, I can't guarantee, but they will come to this kind of a house as readily as to one of the expensive ones.

If you have a barn or shed on your place, nail a 1- by 2-inch board onto one of the horizontal beams (at least six feet above the ground, where a cat can't get to it), and you might lure in a barn-swallow family. This bird likes barns that are in the open, but avoids these in tree groves. Barn swallows attach their nests to the sides of beams wherever there is any bit of a cleat for a footing, including on an electric light socket.

Put up some owl houses (same model as a bluebird house, but bigger—with a two-inch diameter hole). If squirrels take up residence, think squirrel stew. Screech owls are wonderful mouse controllers and take readily to birdhouses. If you happen upon a hollow log, cut it up in about two-foot sections, nail a board over the top and another on the bottom, cut a hole of the appropriate size in the bark, and you have a birdhouse for every occasion.

Don't forget nature's own birdhouses. Many older trees that are far from dead develop thick dead limbs or stubs of limbs. Do not prune out this seeming dead weight. That's where smaller birds find their little hollows for nests and winter shelter. And do not cut down hollow trees that are not likely to fall on houses or fences—they make homes for woodpeckers. The more woodpeckers you have around, the fewer pests such as coddling moth in apples. Keep a bird feeder over winter, and stock it with sunflower seeds. You will lure downy woodpeckers at least, red-breasted and red-headed woodpeckers if any are in your neighborhood, and perhaps hairy woodpeckers. All of them also like to eat bugs hiding under the bark of your fruit trees.

### Bats

Also available from catalogs now, or to make on your own, are bat houses. Bats are great insect predators. When we built our barn, we unwittingly built bat houses, too. To secure the rafters together at the apex of the roof, I had nailed triangular plywood plates to both sides of the joined rafter 2 x 6s. The two-inch space between the two plates on each set of rafters, high above the cats, was quickly commandeered by the bats. I often wonder, where did they live before?

### Toads

If you have a garden pond, you should get lots of toads in your garden. Fired clay toad shelters are now available from garden stores for toads to hide in during the day—a good birthday present for the gardener who has everything. I don't know how to lure garter snakes and spotted salamanders, though in our case, mulch-bed gardening seems to be the charm.

### Dogs

A good dog that will stay in your yard and not bark all night can do wonders for rabbit, squirrel, and coon problems. A fellow I used to know who had a grove of English walnut trees next to Lake Erie (which protected them at frost time) finally almost gave up on trying to harvest a crop, because of squirrels. Then he found a dog that was absolutely death on all rodents. The dog couldn't climb trees, but would actually tree the squirrels after they came from an adjacent woodlot on a nut raid. The nut trees were too young to have hollows in them that squirrels could live in. Once treed, the squirrels could then be (pssst) shot, or scared so bad that if they escaped bullets and dog jaws, they were not so quick to return. Incidentally, you can now get radio-controlled collars for your dog to assist in training him or her to stay on your property. I dream of the day of great progress when technology will put into my hands a radio-activated zapper that I can aim at rabbits, squirrels, neighbor dogs, and Bible hawkers, and urge them on to where they are more appreciated.

### Don't Bother with Gadgets

All those concoctions that rely on odor or noise or sight or taste to scare off wild animals are either worthless, or have an effective life span of two hours to two days. Hungry animals are smarter than you ever imagined.

As for unwanted bugs, those ultraviolet-colored electric bug-zappers have been tested many times by independent researchers, and have always been pronounced ineffective against mosquitoes and flies, and harmful to beneficial night-flying moths. Mosquitoes and flies are always worse in the humid, heavy weather preceding rain, and not so bad for a couple of days after a cold front moves through or on breezy days. Concentrate your outside work during those latter periods.

I loved the recent movie about the pig, Babe, because it depicted the kind of life I love and try to live. But I fear that humanizing animals will do more harm than good to our current cultural attitudes toward the food chain. It is easy to empathize with Babe when he finds out that most pigs are slaughtered for human food. Just remember: In the real world, if a human baby falls into a pig pen, a real Babe will eat it.

# CHAPTER 9

# WATER GARDENING

The most enjoyable change of pace on our homestead is tending to our little garden pond. Located in the meadow behind the tree grove, the pond measures only about forty feet in diameter, with a little extension at one end to make it roughly pear-shaped. The whole pond would fit easily in many backyards. We had it dug in a day with a little bulldozer for $500. The pond builder used a front-end loader to pile the excavated dirt into a little hillock on the westerly side of the pond. Now grassed, the mound acts as a sort of windbreak to increase the comfort of pond-watching on cool, windy days. Others I know who have built ponds in this manner, only bigger, pile the dirt judiciously around two or three sides of the pond to screen it from public view.

The model I used was a tiny pond in the backyard of a suburban home on the edge of a nearby village. The owner was a woman who wrote about nature under the name of Grandma Tellmie. She was (still is, actually) a vivacious and tireless naturalist who could find almost as many adventures with nature in her yard, and the undeveloped land behind it, as Livingston did in traversing the wilds of Africa. She often entertained children, using her home as a living classroom; her backyard pool, with its aquatic life and the creatures it lured to her yard, acted as a blackboard. All the fish had personal names, and they followed her, like pet cats, around the pond edge when she walked by. They could distinguish her from visitors. They hung back shyly under the water plants when I approached. Though the pool was hardly four feet deep at the center, so grandchildren could swim more safely and she herself could cool off with a quick dip after working in the garden, the fish survived winters just fine. (A foot of pea gravel and sand on the floor of the pool kept bathers from stirring up mud.) The shallowness of the pond was a surprise to me, since the expert advice maintains that a pond in this part of northern Ohio should measure eight feet at its deepest point for survival of over-wintering native fish.

A cistern water hauler (we still have such in this rural area) had filled her pool partially. Then rain and runoff from the lawn that sloped gently toward the pool, and a dribbling hose from a faucet to add oxygen as well as water, supplied the rest and maintained the water level. (Such a pool can easily be filled and replenished by channeling the rainwater from a nearby house or garage roof.) Since the land behind her backyard was neither chemicalized farmland nor chemicalized lawn, she did not have to worry about polluted water running into the pool.

Before selecting the site for our pond, I spent several years watching how and where the water ran on our place after a heavy rain. Such a small pond needed enough reliable and clean runoff water from rain to fill up and stay more or less full, but not so much as would flood the pond badly and flush the fish out. I wanted only an excavated pond, not a dammed pond. (A dam requires much more technical expertise and expense to design and build properly, whereas an excavated pond is a simple hole in the ground.) We kept the banks fairly steep (roughly a three-to-one slope) to discourage shoreline weeds. Every time the little bulldozer climbed up from the bottom, I feared it would go end over end, backward, but the operator only laughed at my apprehension.

My main goal was modest: to produce twenty fish dinners every year, or about 40 fish weighing about one and a half pounds. A rule of thumb among commercial fish farmers is that a one-tenth acre pond with supplemental aeration can handle 1,500 to 2,000 fish up to about two pounds in weight. My pond, with a radius of twenty feet, contained roughly one-thirtieth of an acre. That would mean the pond could handle at least 500 fish. But I didn't want to use supplemental aeration, and following my old rule of thumb for chickens—that I would my give animals five to ten times more room than commercial producers do—I lowered my calculated capacity down to 75 to 100 fish total, not counting small fry that would be preyed on by the bigger fish. That would be enough to provide a steady 40 fish per year to eat, with still plenty left to reproduce. I need a couple more years to verify these figures, but they are so conservative that if the fish multiply to twice this number, I'll still be okay.

Then I calculated from the other end of the size spectrum. A rule of thumb among water-garden enthusiasts states that a little pool, three feet by five feet and about two feet deep, can handle 10 to 12 goldfish or koi (carp) six inches long, and more if supplemental aeration is used. That size pool holds roughly 300 gallons of water (formula for an ovalish or rectangularish pool: width × length × depth × 6.7 gallons.) My pool, figuring a diameter of forty feet and an average depth of five feet (formula for a circular pool: diameter × diameter × depth × 5.9 gallons), holds very roughly 50,000 gallons, or about 150 times more than a three- by five-foot garden pool. So it could handle approximately 1,700 six-inch goldfish. Cut this sum by at least half, following my conservative rule of thumb about allowing more space than commercial guidelines state (goldfish can endure a temporary deficiency of oxygen much better than bass can), and we're down to around 800 six-inch fish. But since I want to be eating fish two to three times larger than six inches long, I divide by three and arrive at about 270 fish. So, roughly, I figure the capacity of my pool to be somewhere between 100 and 270, more or less. (You can see that I'm not what you'd ever want to call a precise scientist.)

We dug in August, usually our driest month, so as not to have to contend with mud. Our soil is clay that gets heavier the deeper we dig, so we knew the pond would hold water without a plastic liner. Plastic liners are great for small pools, but they get pricey for a pond forty feet across.

The rains of September quickly filled the pond to overflowing, and after three years, we haven't had any problems. Runoff water after heavy rains from several acres continues to flow over the area as it always did, only now it goes into and out of the pond. A drainage tile through the little meadow carries more water into the pond. I have a bit of screen (actually an old barbecue grill) standing on edge at the point of outflow, to keep the fish from flushing out, but even before I put it in, only tadpoles—not the fish—swam out. We spent our spare time over two succeeding Augusts lining the banks with big flat rocks from a stone quarry. The rocks, which go down into the water a couple of feet, make the pond more attractive, and protect its banks from wave erosion and from the hooves of sheep and cows that have access to the water at certain times. I also lined the bottom of the shallow end (the stem end of the pear shape) with flat rocks, so we could walk out to the deeper water without walking in mud. These rocks, especially the ones along the banks, also protect minnows that the bass would otherwise quickly eat entirely out of the pond. As it turns out, the top rocks also protect the banks from wild Canada geese, who would otherwise trample them to mud and manure. (A Canada goose can excrete up to a pound of manure per day.)

I waited a year before stocking any fish, until some natural life for food and oxygen (such as filamentous algae) had established itself. The algae appeared very soon—a process I don't claim to understand. Within a year, a cattail grew up, which surprised and pleased me. Cattails can take over ponds, but on a small one like mine, I can allow only one small patch and cut out the rest by hand. I expect that in time, a muskrat will take up residence and do this job for me. While controlling pond weeds, and again while lining the banks with rocks, I was well rewarded for keeping the pond so small. Anything larger would present more labor than my back or time could handle.

I pulled a yellow water-lily root out of the creek, where a big patch of these plants has always grown, even back into my childhood, and buried it at the shallow end of the pond across from the cattails. It grew immediately, and spread and bloomed the next year. The water lilies also will have to be kept cut back to prevent them from taking over. They and the cattails offer food and cover for water bugs, bluegills, frogs, and turtles. I plan to eventually introduce some native white water lilies, too, and other water-loving wild plants such as wild iris and cardinal flower on the banks, and perhaps a little arrowhead. I have contemplated water hyacinth, which is a terrible pest plant in the South, but does not overwinter here and so can be used safely as a pond clarifier. However, it spreads fast, so I haven't made up my mind yet. The water has remained fairly clear on its own, and in the fall gets so clear that I can count the fish.

Watching and helping nature fill the new pond with life has been a most absorbing pastime. Lots of work doesn't get done on time around here because we spend so much time sitting at the edge of the pond.

The first noticeable sign of life was a flurry of black water bugs. They were water boatmen, so called because they move about by using their arms (or legs) exactly like oars. Skate bugs, as we call them, appeared soon after, scooting on the water surface. Green frogs arrived next. Then came a flurry of dragonflies and damselflies.

The second year, we stocked about twenty largemouth bass that my son and I caught at another pond, and later I added a couple of hybrid bluegills, a few perch, and shellcrackers (red-eared sunfish)—all good eating, which I purchased at Fender's Fish Hatchery in Baltic, Ohio. The shellcrackers are supposed to keep snails from overpopulating. The largemouth bass are supposed to keep bluegills from overpopulating. And contrary to what I'd read, Mr. Fender insisted that perch do very well in farm ponds. "Just ask any Amish family in Holmes County if you don't believe me," he said. "They all keep perch in their ponds." I tend to believe Mr. Fender, because he told me my fish would not eat the common pelleted fish foods available from grain elevators, and he was right.

Shortly after we stocked the pond, something (I think our cat) caught one of the fish, ate half, and left half on the shore. As far as I can tell, the rest have survived two winters and one drought, when the water level dropped two feet, without supplemental mechanical oxygenation. In a small pond, oxygen is as much of a limiting factor as food. The algae and other water plants have so far provided enough oxygen. In winter, I have religiously pushed the snow off a patch of the ice to let sunlight reach the algae underneath, which the experts say is the thing to do to avoid fishkills. As I cleared snow, I was again thankful for the smallness of our pond.

Just as I'm not sure where the fish get enough oxygen, I don't know what or whether they eat through the long, cold days. As I said, they will not eat commercial pelleted fish food. They sometimes grab a pellet, but then spit it out and glare at me in mild disapproval. In warm weather, they want worms and insects. But going into November, they lose interest even in worms. Mystified, I cut a hole in the ice in January, and with a homemade plastic dipper nailed to a long stick, scooped water off the bottom of the pond and filled a jar with it. To my surprise, the water was full of tiny, barely visible creatures, which under the microscope looked something like miniscule lobsters. Also in the water were a few green hairs, which turned out to be algae. In the house, on the windowsill, the jar of water fairly pulsed with life. The water fleas (I believe that's what they are called) did not die out until March, and the several green hairs multiplied to about twenty and moved about in the jar, eventually coming together in a sort of unbraided rope. When I examined them closely, I saw that they were exuding tiny air bubbles. Evidently millions of these hairs, even in the January pond, were supplying the fish with oxygen. And I assume the fish were eating the tiny water bugs too, enough to stay alive in their semi-hibernation.

When the weather warms up in spring, the fish become very active. In the first year, a school of tiny perch minnows hatched in the brushy safety of last year's Christmas tree, now shorn of its needles, which Mr. Fender had instructed me to put in the pond to protect little fish enough so that big fish had to work harder to catch them. I had visions of platters heaped with perch fried in beer and cornmeal batter. But I don't think any of the fry survived the cavernous jaws of the largemouth bass. At that time, I did not have the rock riprap around the pond edges for them to hide in. Later I caught a few bluntnose minnows from the creek and put them in the pond for the bass to eat, hoping to distract them from the perch. I watched a bass chase one of the bluntnoses literally right out of the water and catch it when it came back down. But a few of these minnows survived by learning to hide in the rocks. I hope they will increase and provide the bigger fish with more food.

The oddest incident in my pond-watching to date happened when a mating pair of dragonflies fluttered over the water. The female was doing all the flying, while the male, its duty done I presume, clung stubbornly to its mate's abdomen as it died. The female kept making clumsy, burdened passes over the pond, each time getting closer to the water surface. Finally it dipped down until the dangling male touched water and then *bam!,* a striking largemouth nipped the male clean away in a quicksilver flash of motion. The female then went merrily on her way, as if she and the largemouth had planned the whole thing. Perhaps they had.

By the third year, algal growth began to thicken on the pond surface. This is good for the fish while the algae is growing and providing oxygen, but can deplete the oxygen when the algae dies and starts rotting. It also can literally fill up a small pond. So for awhile, one of my tasks (a pleasant one really because the pond is small) was to clean out some of the algae once a week during late summer. I used a long sapling pole, sliding it along the surface of the water through the mass of floating algae, or skimmed the water with a manure fork. The algal bloom caught on the pole or fork tines, and dropped off when I swung it over the bank. The dried algal material made good mulch for the garden (see chapter 4).

Water grasses also invaded the pond in the third year. Because they are rooted in the pond bottom, they wouldn't skim off like algae. I had to get in the water and pull them out by hand. Most pond owners dread these grasses and try to get rid of them with various chemicals. The best chemical solution is a (reportedly) harmless blue dye, which darkens the water until it looks like the Mediterranean Sea. The darkened water discourages sunlight, and so discourages weed growth on the pond bottom.

But I found a better remedy, for both the weeds and the algae. I purchased a couple of sterile white amur grass carp from Freshwater Fish of Ohio in Urbana, Ohio. I figured two would be enough ($10 each) for a pond as small as mine, and the friendly folks at Freshwater Fish agreed. Since I already had largemouth bass in the pond, the white amurs needed to be at least eight inches long so the bass wouldn't eat them. In China, these carp are kept in ponds and fed grass like domesticated animals. They can grow to quite large size—I have seen some in a friend's pond that weigh at least five pounds—and are said to be good eating, unlike the Egyptian rough carp that is a pest of our streams and rivers. Also unlike rough carp, the triploid white amur is sterile, and can't become a pest if it escapes a pond.

In short order, the two grass carp cleaned up all the weeds and then the algae. They might keep the pond *too* clean for my purposes, in which case we'll eat one of them.

Last spring, a tribe of toads showed up early at the pond, singing and mating, and strewing the water at the edge of the pond with long, jelly-like strings of eggs. All through April and May, thousands of tadpoles wiggled along the shore. If they ventured out into any water depth at all, the fish got them. When the pond overflowed from spring rain, many tadpoles overflowed, too. I captured most of them with a little net and put them back in the pond. Many hundreds survived to become tiny toads, their tadpole tails suddenly shrivelling up and legs just as suddenly appearing. The fish ate the little toads, as did the bullfrogs, which arrived that summer. Great blue herons also began frequenting the pond, and also ate the little toads. Still, hundreds of tiny toads sifted in to the grass of the field, dodging hawks and snakes. Some made it to adulthood. Now we have lots of them bouncing around the garden.

I have also introduced crayfish into the pond for the bass and for snapping turtles. It might be a mistake to lure in snapping turtles: They are even more voracious eaters than largemouth bass, and will eat anything that moves that they can get into their mouths. But snapping turtles make superb eating. As a matter of fact, so do crayfish. They are miniature lobsters, from a gourmet's point of view.

The largemouth bass have grown slowly so far because of the limited amount of food naturally available to them, but as the food supply grows, especially of their own fry and that of the sunfish, they will grow faster. Bass will eat about anything they can catch. I've read that they will even leap out of the water and grab low-flying songbirds. They consume lots of toad tadpoles and smaller frogs . One bass swam around for days with a large frog stuck in its craw before finally regurgitating it.

The bullfrogs will eat small fish and small frogs, too. We will eat some of the bullfrogs if they increase and multiply enough. In the meantime, I keep increasing the amount of worms and crickets I throw into the pond. To catch crickets and grasshoppers, I swish a butterfly net (homemade from an old curtain) over the clover that grows around the pond. The worms come out of the mulch beds. We hope this fall to taste our first fish dinners.

We have to experiment our way slowly along, learning as we go. I can't emphasize too much the heavenly taste of truly fresh fish from unpolluted water. If our largemouth bass taste as good as the ones we've caught from other ponds, think how wonderful yellow perch—a gourmet fish—will taste. We will need to keep catching and eating the fish (as if that were a problem), because in a small pond it is imperative to keep the population from outrunning the oxygen supply. In tinier garden pools, a third the size of ours, supplemental oxygen is probably necessary if you intend to raise fish to eat.

The latest newcomers to our pond are Canada geese. A pair of them has given every inclination of nesting somewhere nearby. At first I chased them away, because these big honkers can bare the banks and muddy the water of a little pond like ours. Then I decided to let them alone. If they nest, I want to pilfer a fresh goose egg and make an omelet. Goose eggs are supposed to be delicious, and so big that one will make an omelet for two people. The state law allows landowners to break the eggs of this quacking overpopulating pest, but not to shoot the adults—which strikes me as oddly illogical. (In Rockland County, New York, in the summer of 1995, about two hundred overpopulating geese were caught, sent to the slaughterhouse, and their meat given to needy families. Animal-rights activists filed a lawsuit. I'm sorry, that is just stupid. If the meat is not contaminated, and there is no reason why it should be, eating it is exactly the right thing to do.)

Another water-gardening possibility that people used to take much more advantage of than today is the mallard duck. Duck eggs are just as delicious as chicken eggs. Mallards are supposed to be wild, but they readily domesticate if raised from ducklings. When I was a boy, a grizzled old boozer whom Dad referred to as a sourdough always had a flock of mallards quacking around his barnyard, because he strewed corn around his pond. The ducks flew in and stuck around as long as they found corn available. In the fall, however, when the migrating flocks would pass overhead, the home quackers flew off with them, following instinct. In spring, they would show up again on Sourdough's pond, which was really just a large hog wallow, and like wayward husbands would come tiptoeing around the house, hoping for something to eat. Eventually they'd hatch out a brood, and so continue the duckling wheel of life. In this way, old Sourdough had eggs and occasional duckling dinners, without doing a thing except throwing a little corn on the ground. He never worked at anything on his tumbledown farm, except on his ginseng patch. That was the beauty of it all. Cash from the ginseng and a fitful income from haphazard scratching at farming was all the money he needed. We all felt sorry for his wife, whom Mom said was highbred and deserved better. But she never complained, that we ever heard. I remember her milking her cow right out in the field, her scraggly white hair blending into the summer morning mist. Unlike today, when we must all be very efficient just to make sure there's bread on the table, Sourdough and his wife did not work hard, were not ambitious, but ate as well as the rich. Probably better. They had perfected a way to have their duck eggs and eat them, too.

One of our neighboring families today has a pond by their barn and ducks in their trees. A huge black oak grows next to the house, and the ducks actually roost on the broad, nearly horizontal branches. I asked if the family had a favorite way of preparing roast duck. "Oh heavens, we'd never eat them. They're our pets," said the wife. Then she thought a little bit. "Well, we have eaten some. You should not cook them in their own juices. Too greasy. But ducklings are very good otherwise. So are the eggs."

A barrel on its side, close to the water, will sometimes tempt a wild duck or goose to nest, and will certainly serve as shelter and nest for domestic breeds. Wood ducks, too small and far too beautiful to kill, can often be lured to a solitary pond by inserting a specially designed house on a pole in the pond. Wildlife officials will be only too glad to give you directions for making these houses, if they don't have one on hand to give you. If you have a tree with a bare branch high up over the water, you are likely to get a kingfisher to help you thin the ranks of small fry in the water. The kingfisher likes to dive into the water from such a perch. If the tree limbs out over the water are alive and fully leaved, you are likely to find a Baltimore oriole nest swinging from one of them.

So far I've described only what are called warm-water ponds, and the best kind of fish and other animals for them. Where springs exist, homeowners (even in semi-suburban settings) have excavated ponds to take advantage of this source of cold, more or less unpolluted water. In them you can raise trout, certainly a fish high on everybody's list of delicacies. Since most springs deliver a steady and not overabundant supply of water, building a small dam and overflow on the outflow side of the spring-fed pond is a relatively easy job. Freeze-up is not usually a problem with spring-fed ponds, since the water usually doesn't freeze at the upper end, close to the spring's source. The pond still ought to be six to eight feet deep, however, to keep the water cool in summer.

A spring also provides the opportunity to grow watercress, a delicacy you can enjoy in winter. Friends of ours have a sidehill spring that would make a wonderful little pond, but they are not interested. They planted watercress in the little stream that gurgles slowly down the hill from the spring site to a creek, and now the stream is literally choked with the delicious salad green. Unfortunately, since the coming of a nearby housing development served by septic tanks, my friends are afraid to eat the watercress. I argue that if washed well, the cress is safe. It will not draw harmful bacteria into the leaves even if any are present. I munch on some to prove the point, but I don't win the argument.

Even it you aren't interested in the food possibilities of water gardening, a garden pool should contain both fish and plants to be successful. Ecological balance demands this, both from the standpoint of the nitrogen cycle and photosynthesis. The nitrogen cycle maintains the fertility that provides food for both plants and fish. The fish excrete their waste into the water. Nitrifying bacteria in the water convert the waste to a nitrogen-rich fertilizer that the plants and algae can use to grow. The plants then become food for fish directly, or indirectly as food for tinier animals that eventually become food for fish. Death does not mean loss in a pond, since whatever dies only adds to the nitrogen cycle.

Plants and fish help each other "breathe" in the process of photosynthesis. Plants breathe by "inhaling" carbon dioxide and "exhaling" oxygen. Fish inhale oxygen and give off carbon dioxide. Sunlight generates this wonderful partnership, which is why you don't want to leave heavy snow on ice blocking the sun's rays.

I sit by my pond and think about this wonderful symbiotic relationship of animal and plant. Of course, the process goes on outside the pond too, although in air the closeness of the partnership is not as easily perceived. Nature's manufacturing system is unimaginably more efficient than anything man can devise. Our attempts at food production, which our measly science hails as so efficient, are crude and clumsy by comparison. In fact, our manipulations of nature end up being destructive, because they allow us to ignore the delicate population balance, at least for awhile. Such a denial in the pond would bring almost instant retribution.

A major fascination with a water garden is that it is never finished. If I add one new water plant to my pond every year, I will run out of years before I run out of plants. I'm tempted to start listing all the wondrously beautiful plants and fish you can buy from water-garden supply houses. But you will need to get a catalog or two anyway, and then you will be overwhelmed with the selections and the amount of information available. Every conceivable aid to water gardening is offered, including plastic and fiberglass pool shapes of various sizes that you can easily insert into your yard, along with various little artificial waterfall and stream systems that look amazingly real when installed. You can grow a miniature water garden in a fiberglass patio tub, in fact. And most companies offer material and know-how not just for the tiniest pools, but for "wildlife ponds" like ours, with a "bog garden" around the edges, if you wish. Look in the classified ads in garden magazines for sources of water-gardening catalogs. Paradise Water Gardens (14 May Street, Whitman, Massachusetts 02382) and Lilypons Water Gardens (P.O. Box 10, Buckeystown, Maryland 21717) are two well-known sources.

You can spend a lot of money on water gardening, needless to say. Some of the hybrid water lilies cost $40 each. Sophisticated filtering systems that keep the water crystal clear are just as expensive as those meant for swimming pools. But if you use your head and enlarge on some of the methods I've described, you can make a marvelous little pool for little money. If you do spend a bunch, it will buy more satisfying and beneficial relaxation than pounding down the highways, hoping the one you're on is not detoured ahead for repairs. And home improvements represent a lasting investment. Money spent on the road is gone.

Many families are now embracing the idea of transforming their backyards into scenic wonders as the prospect of future travel becomes less and less predictable or affordable or even desirable. Another garden lover and writer, Mary Swander (co-author with Jane Anne Staw of *Parsnips in the Snow,* Iowa, 1990), told me the other day that when people raise their eyebrows at her openly-declared dislike for travel, she quotes her grandmother, who was also loathe to leave her garden. "No, I don't travel anymore," she would say. "I've seen enough scenery."

# CHAPTER 10

# THE AIM IS JOY

I've taken lovely weekend vacations over the years, but the latest one, at an exclusive hideaway we were lucky enough to know about, had to be the best ever. My idea of a good vacation is one that combines natural wonders with good food (the greatest natural wonder of all), hopefully convenient to exhibitions or programs of art or history not yet widely publicized, and so removed from the possibility of crowds and traffic jams. Places that offer such a rare combination are few and far between, and simply discovering this magical retreat was a keen pleasure.

I don't know where to begin in telling you the delights of this vacation. We awoke on Saturday morning to a pervasive silence, broken only by the song of a wood thrush outside our window. We dined on an upper deck, where a flaming orange and black Baltimore oriole scolded us from a huge oak tree whose limbs reached out almost to our table. At one point, the blue flash of an indigo bunting streaked across the orange flame of oriole, and I jumped in delight. That so startled the lovely lady vacationing with me that she lost the strawberry she was spooning from her saucer, and the fruit bounced into the cream pitcher. Giggle, giggle. The strawberries came directly from the establishment's own garden. Yeasty homemade bread also originated in the kitchen, and the eggs were fresh from a nearby barn—we could actually hear the hens cackling. The thick strips of drug- and hormone-free, hickory-smoked bacon came from hogs raised in that barn, too.

We decided to go bird-watching that morning, encouraged by the variety of birds we saw just from the breakfast table. We did not see the bobolinks rumored to have returned to the fields behind the hideaway, but I did spot a stocky lestes (*Lestes dryas*), a species of damselfly, resting in the meadow grass. Though lestes is not exactly an uncommon species in these parts, I had never seen this striking insect before. Its clear lacy wings spread out about an inch and a half; its body was nearly as long. Its abdomen, a little thicker than a darning needle, glinted metallic green in segments marked off by tiny black and whitish bands. Its thorax was shiny green on top, yellowish on the sides shading into rusty brown underneath. Its bulbous eyes were blue, and between them on the back of the prothorax, a yellow and black design, resembling somehow a monkey face, seemed to stare menacingly up at me. In front of the eyes, precise yellow and green lines marked the real mouth parts. What a fearsome sight the damselfly must appear to a mosquito.

We spent the afternoon sunbathing beside the large garden pool on the premises, grateful just to loaf after a week spent sweating and grunting through hay-making. It would be wrong to say that my lovely and I had the pool entirely to ourselves, because we shared it with several species of bass and sunfish that we could see idling in the clear water, plus a green frog floating on a lily pad, four species of dragonflies that I could not name until I fetched my bug book, an Eastern tiger swallowtail butterfly, and several barn swallows skimming over and occasionally touching the water surface. A Canada goose flew near, spotted us, squawked, and barreled away—upset, I suppose, to find what it considered to be its hideaway blasphemed by humans. I decided to take an inventory of all the animals and plants around and in the water, making up names whenever I didn't know the proper one. One dragonfly I called the black and white bi-winger, because it reminded me of a biplane. My lovely laughed and shook her head.

Well, what does it mean to know the "right" name for something? Finding out that the black and white bi-winger was "really" called the white tail, or *Plathemis lydia*, meant only that I could communicate to other humans who knew that name (surely less than 1 percent of the population), and so knew which dragonfly I was talking about. Big deal. Knowing the label did not mean that I knew anything essential about the insect, yet if I could nod toward it and utter *Plathemis lydia* with sober studiousness, I would be considered well informed. That was the pretense in almost all schooling: that memorizing labels meant attaining knowledge.

My rather pompous declaration led to an argument in which my lovely maintained that all language was labeling, and labeling was necessary, because if we did not agree on which word stood for what, all communication would turn into chaotic babbling. I countered (having no way to win the argument, of course) by pointing out that all communication by way of labeling had turned into chaotic babbling anyway, and I could hear more truth in the vibrating hums of damselfly wings than in the electronic hums of television advertisements. As I exhorted on the subject, she fell asleep.

I baited a fishing line and casually cast into the pool. *Wham!* A large-mouth bass struck almost before the hook hit the water. As my rod bent, I wondered why I had ever journeyed into faraway fastnesses of northern Minnesota and Canada in search of fishing thrills, when I could have the same pleasure here with a lot less road time. Only "here" was even better: fewer mosquitoes. I caught a second bass just as fast, and reluctantly obeyed the management's request that we limit ourselves to only two—enough for a meal that the house would prepare.

We had not eaten lunch (we would eat the fish next day) so as to do justice to a large evening meal: generous slices of drug- and hormone-free standing rib roast, which had been marinating in the chef's secret formula of spices all day; Bibb lettuce and baby onions, again fresh from the establishment's kitchen garden; finger-sized zucchini squash, roasted lightly over an open grill; more homemade bread, with plenty of butter; and strawberry shortcake, soaked in cream. The finger-sized zucchini were delicious, something I can seldom say about big ones. This was the secret of what to do with "all those zucchini." You are supposed to eat them when they are tiny, and then "all those zucchini" aren't so many after all.

After dinner, we attended a performance of the *Nutcracker Suite*. I really wanted to see a movie (there was a new Western showing), so I tried hard to doze off to make my lovely feel guilty. It didn't work: neither the dozing off, nor the feeling guilty.

Next morning, the Hideaway (I shall call it that) offered a really unique experience: a sort of layman's archeological expedition. Or, more accurately, a treasure hunt. The area was noted for its Stone Age artifacts. Almost anywhere the soil was reasonably clear of vegetation—as in creek beds, along shorelines and river banks, around construction sites, in plowed fields, and between rows in corn fields—flint spear points and arrowheads were sometimes found, along with polished slate and granite hammerheads and hatchets.

Our "expedition" began with a trek up a creek bed, going upstream so the current would sweep the mud stirred by our feet behind us. A carved human head of black granite had reportedly been found in this creek, an extremely unusual artifact for this area, so our expectations were high. Too high. But we did find an old Coca Cola bottle of some small value, which lured us into a ravine running down to the creek where a farm family had dumped its cans and bottles and old fence-wire and other detritus for who knows how many years. This dump was really old, because most of the metal containers had rusted away, leaving only glass objects intact. My lovely found what appeared to be a handblown bottle and we began to paw delightfully and almost savagely through the junk. Treasure-hunting in a dump. Have you any idea how exciting that can be? Ask any bottle collector.

Exhausting the possibilities there without a shovel to dig deeper, we moved on up the brow of a hill overlooking the creek. The land there appeared to have been plowed and then abandoned, or perhaps put in one of those insane farm programs where farmers are paid not to farm. There was not yet much vegetation covering the field. In a bare spot, I found a tiny flint arrowhead shaped like the silhouette of a bird in flight. Although so delicate that it appeared to be as fragile as an egg shell, it had survived the centuries unbroken and ready for use. What do we moderns know about progress? What do we make with that kind of durability? How could any hand have possessed the skill to shape such a delicate thing out of hard, unyielding flint in the first place? What were the odds against my finding it? What was its maker like? Surely this arrowhead was not made to kill anything, but to please someone. And hundreds of years later, it will now find its way into a pendant around my lovely's neck to please yet another.

Caught up in excitement and expectation, we did not realize that morning had passed. We cut a straight line back to the Hideaway, noting and trying to identify the many kinds of wildflowers blooming. Passing through a patch of woodland, we spied one of the most unusual, if not rarest, species in this region: Indian pipe or (studiously) *Monotropa uniflora*. It resembles a smoking pipe in shape, with the bowl end up. Its striking quality is a complete lack of chlorophyll, so that it appears to be a fungus rather than a wildflower. Grayish white in the absence of color, it is also known as ice plant and ghost flower, both names much more appropriate, in my estimation, and much more universally known than *Monotropa uniflora*. Ghost flower is saprophytic, that is, it lives on dead plant life. Part of the folklore that goes with the wildflower is an old belief that it grows where aboriginal Native Americans were buried. With my little arrowhead clenched in my fist, I had no problem with that notion.

The fish I had caught the day before became our meal, filleted, dusted in freshly ground cornmeal mixed into a beer batter, fried, and sautéed with lemon juice. I had so infrequently tasted *truly* fresh fish from unpolluted water that I was almost shocked at the mild, delicate deliciousness of these fillets. I ordered a second helping without batter, so that nothing competed with the pure taste of the fish.

The rest of the afternoon we spent bicycling through the countryside to a tiny village. It was amazing what awaited discovery along these most ordinary and humble byways. We came to a large sign that stated simply but mysteriously: *Rosary.* An arrow pointed to the farmhouse back off the road. Intrigued, we accepted the sign's silent invitation and pedaled down the lane. There, stretched across the yard, hung on fence posts, was (as the owner soon explained) a two-ton rosary! Step aside, Lourdes; is this not a miraculous event worthy of a million tourists? The beads of the rosary were huge blocks of black-walnut wood, measuring about three feet square per side, linked together with strands of log chain. The crucifix at the beginning of the huge rosary had been carved with a chainsaw, also out of black walnut. This was as good an example of folk art as I have seen anywhere, and I have seen quite a bit. No, the farmer said, he had not had any experience in carving or sculpting before, with or without a chainsaw. Inside his house, which he insisted on showing us, a splendid metal sculpture of a flowering vine covered most of the wall above the stone fireplace. He had made the vine out of copper, also without previous experience. He had laid up the fireplace stones himself, too, learning as he proceeded. In fact, he had built the whole house. He had learned how to do that by building barns, he said. Building barns was what he was good at, he told us matter of factly when we praised his artfulness. And fixing motors. About art, he said he didn't know much. I understood then the meaning of the word "artlessly."

He told us if we pedaled on a few more miles, we could find other "sights for sore eyes," such as a large fieldstone grotto that a farmer had laid up in his barnyard, in memory of a son who had died at a young age. And we would come to a village hardware store that also doubled as a sort of local museum. And a "pretty good restaurant" that we could get to without ever confronting a traffic light or more than a half-dozen cars. The village itself, he said, was the kind of place where people going into the grocery store (before it closed for the night) and finding no one there to wait on them, would take what they needed and leave the money on the counter. "Once there were seven saloons in that village," he said with a grin. "One for every seven people in town, if you didn't count all the farmers who lived roundabout in those days and all the Methodists who came from other towns to do their drinking unseen by their neighbors. My father's biggest cash crop was selling ice from his ponds to those saloons."

Unfortunately, we did not have time for such delights, so we pedaled back to the Hideaway and to the end of a thoroughly relaxing and fulfilling weekend.

As you may have guessed, the Hideaway is our own home. All the adventures recounted really did happen as we "vacationed" right in our own neighborhood. We had to fix our own food, of course—where is there a restaurant that could have duplicated our homegrown, home-cooked fare? The *Nutcracker Suite* was on television. We do have unusually intriguing neighbors, but so does everyone if you just take the time to root down and become aware of them.

And that seems to me the way to aim for joy and genuine satisfaction in life. It is not just the idea that contrary gardeners can make of their homes little earthly paradises. Wealthy people build far grander places than most of us can afford, but they occupy their castles only rarely and seem to enjoy them only as marks of their success. Not satisfied, they are constantly in the process of going someplace else to build another castle.

What makes home a place we always leave regretfully and always return to joyfully is the deeper knowledge of Place that the homebody cultivates in the process of creating a little garden paradise. We could not have enjoyed the weekend just described without a very intimate knowledge of our surroundings.

I learned one of the great lessons of my life from Andrew Wyeth, whose paintings have riveted me from the first time I saw one. Then I learned that he had painted all of his world-revered masterpieces within walking distance of where he lives. Talking to him and reading what he said about artistic creativity, I realized that only by a continuously deeper and deeper examination of the familiar could I find real meaning in life, as he did, and thereby gain some genuine satisfaction from it. I became so excited with this new (to me) realization that I thought my skin was going to rip open.

Then I happened upon Wendell Berry's poetry, which affected me the same way that Wyeth's paintings had. Journeying to visit Berry, I found that he too centered almost his entire output of poems, essays, and novels in his little neighborhood farm community.

He had come back home from Europe and New York and all that promise of glitter to a secluded, ruined hillside overlooking the Kentucky River, and had turned it into his own little ecological paradise. From him came the same message: Only the deep familiarity of being rooted a long time in a Place could produce real art, and art—or artfulness—produced joy. In the title essay from his book *The Long-Legged House,* he put it this way: "Here as well as any place I can look out my window and see the world. There are lights that arrive here from deep in the universe. A man can be provincial only by being blind and deaf to his province."

But he said it better perhaps in what became my favorite lines of poetry (from "On a Hill Late at Night," in his *Collected Poems*) after I had my own hillside:

*I am wholly willing to be here*
*between the bright silent thousands of stars*
*and the life of the grass pouring out of the ground.*
*The hill has grown to me like a foot.*
*Until I lift the earth I cannot move.*

Too many of us have been so seduced by the impossible challenge of trying to think "globally" that we turn away from the possible challenge of thinking locally. We become restless and join the crowds of world roamers who never *know*, intimately and particularly, anything at all except the act of roaming. I saw this happening to myself, so I went home. I like what Grant Wood said after he came home from Europe, disillusioned, to become one of our greatest painters: "I realized that all the really good ideas I'd ever had came to me while I was milking a cow." Me too.

I can't explain, to those as yet unrooted, why it is possible for me to walk over our little farm every day and never cease to draw keen pleasure from it. I always see something new, or something old that has changed in a new light, or something old that has not changed, which is the greatest thrill of all. I have gazed in wonder at Grand Canyons along our creek banks and Niagara Falls in the plunge of the creek water over rocks. I have seen a tiny star-nosed shrew swim *underwater* in that creek; great blue herons wade through it, and surpassingly gorgeous wood-ducks floating on it. I have watched a boy all alone and happy, flying down the creek on skates, and a beauteous wood-nymph of a girl emerge from the water, glistening naked in the sunlight. In the wooded hills above the creek, I have been awestruck by tree trunks glowing orange in the setting sun and mushrooms glowing yellow in the moonlight.

If I extend the boundaries of my daily walk beyond our property, and retrace old pathways up the valley to my childhood home—less than two miles distant but sixty years away in time—every turn in that creek, every woodlot hovering above it, every roll of hill down to it, reminds me of some small adventure of my past. I walk along holding hands with all the people of this community, past and present.

The intimacy that brings joy to the contrary gardener feathers out into all spheres of communal activity. Walking down the streets of any one of five nearby villages, I am sure to see a friend, a family member, or at least someone I know well enough to stop and talk to. A village walk becomes a sort of circle dance. I once received a letter addressed to me "Somewhere in Wyandot County, Ohio." When a national newspaper wrote an article about one of our villages, it alluded to this fact by saying that Carey, Ohio, was so intimately small that a letter would get to the right place without a proper address. Some school kids in Georgia did not believe this, so they sent another letter addressed to me "Somewhere in Wyandot County 43316." Once more, the letter found me, and 43316 is not my zip code! Let's see e-mail do that.

This sort of communal intimacy and trust gives me the keenest pleasure. At a local restaurant (Woody's at the edge of Upper Sandusky, where I can drive without confronting a single traffic light), a friend and I fell into such a deep conversation over lunch one day that we did not realize the passing time. Suddenly we were aware that all was dark and quiet around us. Everyone had left for the afternoon, including the waitresses, cooks, and manager. They had just turned the lights out and left us to blab away. They knew we'd make sure the door locked behind us when we left.

Ironically enough, the more one immerses oneself in the complexity of the familiar, the more one can attain simplicity of life. We contrary gardeners often refer to this simplicity as "the simple life," even though we know that its manifestations are simple only by very complex design. Thus we cherish "simple" pleasures:

A sunset;
Rest after hard physical work;
Eating after sharp hunger;
Stripping away anxiety about what we should wear
Until we wear nothing at all;
Gentle rain on the roof after a long drought;
The sound of a violin wafting through the trees,

Of a parent or spouse singing at work,
Of children laughing at play,
Of a thrush at twilight;
The camaraderie of drinking beer after a ballgame;
The radiance of a woodstove after barn chores in winter;
The touch of a drying wind on bare skin after swimming;
The taste of a pullet egg, laid today,
Of a pork chop from a hog butchered and cooled outside
In fresh, crisp, wintry air,
Then grilled over smoldering hickory-bark chips,
Of sweet corn roasted in the late "pimply" stage,
When, if you push your fingernail against a kernel,
It spits corn milk in your eye,
Of boiled lima beans picked "too young,"
No bigger than a fingernail and not much thicker,
Of a new potato the size of a ping-pong ball,
Freshly dug and boiled,
Of beans, baked with a little mustard and brown sugar,
And a thick top layer of home-cured, home-smoked bacon,
Of a winesap apple pie with a lard crust.

Anyone can marvel with passing curiosity at the beauty of a monarch butterfly. But what is that pleasure compared to the awe of contrary gardeners, familiar with the mystery of what they are looking at? Those fragile wings can carry the monarch from Canada to Mexico and back. The insect's jewel-like egg hatches into a misty green, glistening caterpillar that seals itself in a jade-like chrysalis to emerge a year later as an explosion of orange.

But this is only the shallowest part of the mystery. The adult monarch so closely resembles the viceroy butterfly that only an expert can tell them apart. Yet the two insects bear absolutely no resemblance to each other in their other stages of life. The viceroy's larva looks like a bird dropping, and its chrysalis is a brown, almost greasy blob. It eats totally different food in a totally different habitat. As an adult, it does not migrate.

How did the two butterflies come to "evolve" into almost identical twins? The general assumption has been that monarchs, feeding exclusively on bitter milkweed, taste bad to birds, and so after trying to eat one or two, the birds avoid them. Therefore, the viceroy, whose larva feeds on willow leaves and in all stages is apparently tasty to birds, has evolved to look like the monarch to protect itself.

But this reasoning begs a number of very huge questions. Mimicry is the standard form of protection against predators in nature, but it almost always involves blending a given species into its surroundings by camouflage. Bright orange against a blue sky or a green tree is hardly camouflage in the first place, but nowhere else in nature is there an example of an open-flying insect mimicking another open-flying insect, in an almost total disregard of camouflage. Viceroys do not merge into flocks of monarchs to hide themselves; monarchs are off migrating when viceroys need them most. Furthermore, the disparate taste preferences of birds would have had to evolve along with the two disparate butterflies.

So what gives here? A great mystery, that's what gives. No known process of evolution fits the case of the monarch and the viceroy. Consider: If a bird is to avoid a viceroy because it looks like a monarch, it must first eat a monarch and then decide it doesn't like monarchs. This means, in evolutionary logic, that the monarch had to precede the viceroy not only in long-term evolutionary time, but in its yearly life cycle. Monarchs must be flying before viceroys emerge. For such timing and seasonal rhythm to have concurred between two insects with wholly different lifestyles is so remarkable as to defy both logic and evolutionary science. One can as reasonably assume that the twin butterflies are a colossal accident of nature. Or that a God is amusing himself by befuddling the arrogance of humans.

> *I catch a monarch with a torn wing*
> *And stare at it in awe.*
> *Or is it a viceroy I am beholding?*
> *The insect trembles in my open hand.*
> *Or is it my hand trembling?*

# INDEX

## Chelsea Green Publishing Company

The sustainable world is one in which all human activities are designed to co-exist and cooperate with natural processes rather than dominate nature. Resources are recognized as finite. Consumption and production are carefully and consciously balanced so that all of the planet's species can thrive in perpetuity.

Chelsea Green specializes in providing the information people need to create and prosper in such a world.

Sustainable Living has many facets. Chelsea Green's celebration of the sustainable arts has led us to publish trend-setting books about organic gardening, solar electricity and renewable energy, innovative building techniques, regenerative forestry, local and bioregional democracy, and whole foods. The company's published works, while intensely practical, are also entertaining and inspirational, demonstrating that an ecological approach to life is consistent with producing beautiful, eloquent, and useful books, videos, and audio tapes.

For more information about Chelsea Green, or to request a free catalog, call (800) 639–4099, or write to us at P.O. Box 428, White River Junction, VT 05001.

Chelsea Green's titles include:

| | |
|---|---|
| *The Flower Farmer* | Lynn Byczynski |
| *The New Organic Grower* | Eliot Coleman |
| *Four-Season Harvest* | Eliot Coleman |
| *Solar Gardening* | Leandre Poisson and Gretchen Vogel Poisson |
| *Forest Gardening* | Robert Hart |
| *Whole Foods Companion* | Dianne Onstad |
| *The Man Who Planted Trees* | Jean Giono |
| *Loving and Leaving the Good Life* | Helen Nearing |
| *The Straw Bale House* | Athena Swentzell Steen, Bill Steen, and David Bainbridge |
| *Independent Builder* | Sam Clark |
| *The Sauna* | Rob Roy |

## The Garden Alliance

The Garden Alliance consists of companies and organizations supportive of the practices of organic gardening and the principles of sustainable living. Charter members of the Alliance are:

*Johnny's Selected Seeds.* Johnny's was founded in 1974 by Rob Johnston, Jr. The company operates an organic farm in Albion, Maine, and provides its customers with a full line of untreated seeds. Johnny's breeding program has produced AAS award-winning pumpkins and Swiss chard along with a number of unique vegetable varieties. The company maintains the largest trial gardens in the Northeast.

A company that prides itself on their catalog, their quality vegetable, herb, and flower seeds, and their outstanding service, Johnny's is dedicated to the education of gardeners of all ages. The company mission is to "help families and friends to feed one another." Free color catalog available.

Johnny's Selected Seeds
Foss Hill Road, RR1, Box 2580, Albion, ME
207-437-9294    (fax) 207-437-2165
Internet: http://www.johnnyseeds.com

*Seeds of Change.* Seeds of Change is committed to safeguarding personal health and the health of the soil by providing 100 percent certified organic, open-pollinated seeds of the highest quality, including many heirloom, traditional, and unique Seeds of Change varieties. The company grows seeds on their own research farms, and through their special network of family farms in accordance with Oregon Tilth's organic certification standards.

Seeds of Change also works with various communities worldwide to spread the practices of sustainable agriculture, to conserve the plants and agricultural customs particular to those areas, and to exchange germ plasm. They also donate thousands of seed packs annually to school, relief efforts, and prison garden projects.

Organic seeds are available from their full-color catalog, in natural food stores and nurseries, and on their web site.

Seeds of Change
P.O. Box 15700, Santa Fe, NM 87506-5700
888-762-7333   (fax) 505-438-7052
Internet: http://www.seedsofchange.com

*NOFA (Northeast Organic Farming Association).*   NOFA is a non-profit association of consumers, gardeners, and diversified farmers who share a vision of local, organic agriculture. Founded in Vermont, there are now seven independent state chapters. For information about membership in the organization and its certification standards, contact:

NOFA
P.O. Box 697, Bridge Street, Richmond, VT 05477
802-434-4122   Web site: http://www.nofavt.org

*Gardener's Supply Company.*   Gardener's Supply is "America's Gardening Resource." The company offers a broad range of tools, fertilizers, all-natural pest controls, and even products for organic lawn care. Their location in Burlington, Vermont is adjacent to the historic flood plain known as the Intervale, which has become a popular demonstration site of gardening and composting techniques.

The company offers a professional home-study course that can lead to certification as a Master Horticulturist. This enables serious gardeners to learn the fundamentals of plant science and ecology at their own pace and within the comforts of their own homes. Free catalog available.

Gardener's Supply Company
128 Intervale Road, Burlington, VT 05401
800-863-1700   (fax) 800-551-6712
Email: info@gardeners.com
Web site: http://www.gardeners.com